# Autis~

## and

# Learning

A Guide to Good Practice

Edited by
**Stuart Powell**
and **Rita Jordan**

**David Fulton Publishers**
London

David Fulton Publishers Ltd
Ormond House, 26-27 Boswell Street, London WC1N 3JZ

www.fultonpublishers.co.uk

First published in Great Britain by
David Fulton Publishers 1997
Reprinted 1998, 1999, 2000, 2001

**British Library Cataloguing in Publication Data**

A catalogue record for this book is available from the British Library

ISBN 1-85346-421-X

Typeset by Textype Typesetters, Cambridge
Printed in Great Britain by the Cromwell Press, Ltd., Trowbridge

# Contents

This book is dedicated to those with autism and those who educate and care for them

# List of contributors

**Dr Stuart Powell** is Reader in Educational Psychology at the University of Hertfordshire.

**Rita Jordan** is Senior Lecturer in Autism at the University of Birmingham.

**Gina Davies** is a Speech and Language Therapist based at the 'Little Group', Epsom.

**Geoff Evans** is Northern Regional Training Officer for the National Autistic Society, and is based at Storm House School, Rotherham.

**Margaret Golding** is Teaching Fellow at the University of Hertfordshire and was until recently Headteacher of Linden Bridge School, Surrey.

**Sarah Libby** is Research Fellow at the University of Kent at Canterbury and the Centre for Social and Communication Disorders, Bromley.

**Stephanie Lord** is Headteacher of Heathermount School, Ascot, Berkshire.

**Pam Maddock** is Principal of Wargrave House School, Newton-le-Willows, Merseyside.

**Dr Dinah K.C. Murray** is a researcher living and working in London (42 Cheverton Road, London N19 3AZ).

The chapter on Assessment was written by staff at the Helen Allison School, (National Autistic Society) Kent and compiled by **Malcolm Taylor** (Head of the Post-16 Unit).

# Preface

Autism is a complex and puzzling disorder that has attracted many theories concerning its basic nature and numerous claims for therapies or teaching approaches that offer *the* solution. We have argued for an educational approach that takes account of the specific 'autistic' way of thinking and learning (Jordan and Powell, 1995; Powell and Jordan, 1993), but we have never accepted that such a single approach exists and we have urged parents and teachers to take account of the wealth of experience and expertise in educating individuals with autism, that exists within the UK. We have fought shy of offering recipe approaches, however, for we believe that best practice reflects an understanding of the nature of autism (and the capacity to update that understanding as knowledge grows), knowledge of a range of strategies that have been used successfully with people with autism and resources that allow flexibility in their application to meet the different needs of individuals with autism. People with autism are alike in that they share the triad of impairments that underlie the condition (Wing, 1996), but they are also individuals and their difficulties in participating in the process of socialisation may even mean that they are more individualistic and idiosyncratic in their development than other children. If educationists try to follow a 'recipe', then, they will sooner or later come across a child or a situation where the recipe does not work. Without an understanding of what to do and why, they will then find themselves in the same position as the individual with autism: unable to step outside of the learned routine and at a loss as to how to proceed next.

Rather than offer such a step by step guide to 'our approach', we take the view that educationists need to operate at the level of applying principles which are based on a sound understanding of the pedagogy and the psychology of autism. We have found that what practitioners are already doing often falls within what we would consider 'good practice' and that what one needs to do to further improve practice and disseminate it, is to analyse why successful teachers do what they do, what they actually do and what is really happening in terms of results (children's learning). Such an analysis should lead to the kind of improvements that are desired, if it is disseminated effectively. Yet practitioners, in the UK at least, are often caught up in the practicalities of their work and are reluctant to point to a moment in time and say 'Now we have got it right'. They quite rightly perceive that there is always more to learn and improvements to be made. Nevertheless, our experience of going into many different schools in the UK is that many of them have 'got it right', at least in principle. Rather than limiting ourselves to our own experiences, then, we felt our role could be one of analysing that practice we have seen, in terms of underpinning theoretical bases. We felt that it was best to let the practitioners speak for themselves in describing their practice, but that we could offer principles from our analysis that would better enable others to learn from the practice and apply it to their own situation. This book is an attempt to conduct such an analysis.

Nearly all the contributors are practitioners and each describes one aspect of their professional practice. They were asked because, in our understanding, their approach to the teaching of children with autism may loosely be described as falling within the kind of approach that we as editors have researched and advocated in various publications and which has been brought together in *Understanding and Teaching Children with Autism* (Jordan and Powell, 1995). Each contributor was asked to write a chapter describing a particular aspect of their practice in terms of what they do, why they think they do it and what happens when they have done it. They were then asked for a reflective description including information on results. We as editors subsequently added a short commentary showing how the work relates to the theory that we have expounded.

In summary, the book is about how a psychological perspective on the way in which individuals with autism think and learn may be applied to particular curriculum areas. The first chapter by the editors, sets the scene by establishing the broad rationale for our approach and the psychological understanding on which it is based. The second chapter sets out the principles by which this understanding can be translated into practice. The book does not represent *all* the good practice that exists in the UK, nor are we necessarily claiming that it is the best, even of its type. What we have done is chosen a few key areas of curriculum content or delivery where we knew there were good reflective practitioners who would be prepared to share their understanding and practice with others.

## References

Jordan, R.R. & Powell, S.D. (1995) *Understanding and Teaching Children with Autism.* Chichester: Wiley.

Powell, S.D. & Jordan, R.R. (1993) 'Diagnosis, intuition and autism'. *British Journal of Special Education,* **20,** 1, 26–29.

Wing, L. (1996) *Autism Spectrum Disorders.* London: Constable.

CHAPTER 1

# Rationale for the approach

Stuart Powell and Rita Jordan

## Some Basic Premises

This book does not set out to explain autism; we would refer the reader to other texts for that explanation. What we aim to do is to pinpoint some key features in our understanding and interpretation of the condition, that we feel underpin examples of good practice. At the root of our beliefs about the education of those with autism is the notion that we need to respect the way in which those individuals think and learn. By 'respect' we mean more than the acknowledgement of a right to the kind of respect that is necessary in any human relationship if it is to be truly of the *human* kind. We use the term here to include a notion of recognition at a psychological level that the world is as it seems to the individual with autism *for him/her.* We think this holds true in as much as the way in which the child perceives and reacts to the social and physical worlds in which they live represents a reality for him/her. We may not be able to share autistic ways of understanding but that is our problem as teachers and our starting point for any move towards real learning on the part of our students. There is a natural tension (which professionals need to resolve) between, on the one hand, respecting the individual's autism and so working within its constraints, and, on the other hand, trying to enable individuals with autism to work effectively and live productively within the non-autistic world by improving the effectiveness of their thinking and learning.

Having described our intention to report in this book examples of good practice it is important to note here that we do not expect such examples to be flawless. We know that teaching individuals with autism is difficult and that the best laid plans may not prove fruitful. What we would wish is that the difficulties should be recognised and ways of dealing with them considered. In short, what we offer in this book are descriptions of how teaching and learning in autism develops rather than a recital of the 'way it should be done'. We do not want, therefore, to be seen to say, 'Do this and all will be well', but rather to show how to make sense of what the child with autism does and how to build a teaching approach based on this understanding.

What is needed is both a recognition of the real nature of the problem in autism and knowledge of the individual to determine how that 'problem' has affected development in that particular case. Teachers who are not experienced in autism may find it difficult to recognise, let alone teach, the 'achievements' that are part of normal spontaneous processes of learning, since the learning is so early, and so implicit. When working with children with autism, however, such achievements cannot be assumed; they will need to be explicated. What is required then is a truly reflective model of teaching – one in which the teacher engages in a process of reflection on their own learning and reactions as part of their analysis of how the learning situation is for the child with autism and subsequently what they need to do to make that situation more effective for the learner. The danger with a recipe approach to teaching (which we note above that we are seeking to avoid) is that teachers will begin at the second level of this reflection (that is what needs to be done to the situation). In our view the first level (that is, reflection on own learning and how it is for their student) is of primary importance.

We need to recognise, as indicated below, that for many children with autism, especially those with additional learning difficulties, even direct and explicit teaching may not enable them to attain a significant level of understanding. In the chapters of this book, therefore, we have asked contributors to include in their descriptions of practical approaches, the kinds of compensatory strategies that can be taught and which may enable the student to develop intellectually in spite of problems and thereby to gain access to new learning and new ways of behaving. But this leads to another important premise: we should be wary of assuming failure and having low expectations. We would not deny the difficult challenge that autism represents for education nor would we want to claim that we have a 'cure' or even that following the examples given will automatically lead to success. We have had sufficient failures in our own teaching to recognise such claims as false or at least naive. Nevertheless, we have also witnessed remarkable achievements in young people with autism and it is unjust to their efforts and those of their teachers to deny their success or always to claim that 'they couldn't have been that autistic in the first place'. We think that good teaching can make a difference and high expectations (as long as they accept the child's difficulties) are as important in the education of those with autism as for any other group. We cannot always know why one child succeeds and another does not, and we know the difference in outcome is not always because of the way they were taught. Yet we do believe that an optimistic and determined approach, based on sound principles, can make a difference.

## An Educational 'Diagnosis'

It is important to recognise that autism is a developmental disorder and so any initial or fundamental disability will not just have an effect on development equivalent to difficulties resulting from that disability. A blind child does not develop in a way that equals 'normal development minus sight'. Rather, every aspect of development is affected by the switch from visual to other forms of obtaining and processing information; there will be strengths (at least in a relative sense) as well as weaknesses in a congenitally blind child's thinking and learning. Exactly the same will be true of autism so that even if we can identify (or agree) the fundamental disability in autism, the results will not just be in terms of deficits but rather in a different way of thinking and learning – an 'autistic' way.

We also need to remember that autism does not often occur in a 'pure' form; many individuals with autism will have additional difficulties, most commonly, additional general and/or specific learning difficulties. These additional difficulties will in turn constrain the kind of development that takes place and the teaching approaches that can be adopted. We do not distinguish various sub-sets of the autistic spectrum (such as Asperger's Syndrome) in our analyses, partly because we are not convinced of the validity of these sub-divisions as separate syndromes, but also because it confuses medical diagnosis with diagnosis for education. Whether or not there are good medical and scientific grounds for separating different syndromes within the autistic spectrum, we hold the position that it is the commonality of disturbance through the entire spectrum – the triad of impairments (Wing, 1988) that makes autism an important diagnosis educationally. It is the psychological reason for the co-occurrence of that pattern of diagnostic features that makes it autism and that makes for a characteristic unique learning style.

Of course, we do not mean to deny that differences in general cognitive ability and in the degree of language ability will have enormous implications for the development of the child. However, these differences need to be accounted for in one's consideration of the individual aspects of each child's development, rather than in considering the implications of their autism. The chapters in this book, then, do not necessarily specify a particular 'autistic population' to which they refer. In most cases, the children dealt with will cover the spectrum of ability and, where particular approaches are most suited to a particular general or language ability level, this will be indicated.

## Propositions Underlying our Understanding of Autism

In this section we formulate a conceptual framework which is intended to be in the first place explanatory of autism and in the second indicative of possible effective educational approaches. We will suggest that there are four key interconnected features of autistic thinking: firstly the way in which information is perceived, secondly the way in which the world is experienced, thirdly the way in which information is coded, stored and retrieved in memory, and finally the role of emotion as a context in which those processes may or may not operate. It is neither possible nor appropriate to give the full research and theoretical base of our position here; we state our position, not to argue for it as fact, but to enable the reader to grasp the rationale for our approach. It is interesting that many of our principles might derive from other understandings of autism, and it is not necessary for the reader to subscribe fully to our understanding of autism to find value in the practical approaches given in this book.

## Perception

It is clear from the writings of many high functioning individuals with autism that stimuli from the environment are not perceived in the same way as is the case for the majority of non-autistic individuals. Accepting that everyone, in one sense, perceives things in their own way and that there will be individual differences across a range of kinds of stimuli, it is clear that the degree of commonality that is found in the non-autistic population is not present in the autistic. What is initially striking is that across the range of the five senses there is not the regularity of perception in individuals with autism that typifies the non-autistic way of perceiving. Some of this may result from abnormalities in interpreting sensory information and some from the failure of socialisation to provide a specific social and cultural meaning for what is perceived. Often it is difficult to distinguish the two. If the child with autism is unable to selectively attend to verbal instructions in the classroom, is that because the auditory signal fades in and out and is thus inherently difficult to attend to (as some able people with autism have claimed) or is it because verbal information has no special social or cultural significance and so it is no more salient than the sound of a distant fan or the feel of the clothes on the skin? If speech is not meaningful, then the child will not be practised at paying attention to it in preference to what we would normally classify as 'background' stimulation.

So, to the child with autism, particular sounds and the feel of materials, for example, may shift over time in terms of the intensity with which they are perceived. That is true for us all, but for the majority there is more conscious directing of our attention, and social stimuli (such as the teacher's instructions) are usually more salient unless other stimuli are insistent (a pain, for example), persistent (the increasing uncomfortableness of a hard chair as we sit through a long lecture) or charged with emotional impact (fear from a phobic reaction to a spider we have just seen). All these factors are also important in the direction of attention in autism, but people with autism appear to have more difficulty in perceiving in uniform ways, and in attaching social or personal meaning to what they see (or hear; the evidence for the proximal senses is unclear). Regularity is one of the necessary features of learning. The child in the cot learns about the world precisely because things happen with regularity (when they cry someone comes and makes particular kinds of response); it is this regularity that enables them to begin to make predictions – if I cry then someone will come. Certainly, the example we have given may be a primitive non-cognitive behaviour, but it is one which is built upon to form early learning. And, again, the essential building block is regularity and hence predictability. If the child with autism has difficulty perceiving the regularities 'out there' in the world or in sharing a view of the world where these patterns are literally pointed out and given meaning, then it is not surprising if they seek to impose regularity and predictability by the stereotyped ordering of their world.

So, if a regular sense of perception that is commonly shared with others is so central to learning, it becomes clear that in autism that process of learning will be impaired. The question arises, as we have indicated, as to whether perceptual irregularities in autism create conceptual problems or whether in fact it is conceptual problems in the first place that have created the perceptual irregularities. Clearly, the relationship between concept and percept is a transactional one; both develop through an interaction with the other. If you have no conception of the meaning of *hammer* then the object lying on the table remains just that and this 'object' can only be described in terms of what is conceptually available to the individual (perhaps for example: 'a piece of wood with a piece of metal stuck across the top'). On the other hand if you cannot achieve a constant image of the object which can be shared with others and thus established as the tool we know as *hammer* then it will be difficult to develop a conceptual understanding.

This becomes even more problematic when considering concepts of the self and other. As Hobson (1993) has argued, infants have to have some idea that they belong to the same kind of class as others (that is, that they are all persons) before they can start attributing emotions, thoughts, intentions, to others, on the basis of analogy with their own. Is it the cognitive capacity to make the analogy that is missing in autism (as some theorists claim) or is it the initial intuitive perception of a person that would make the analogy possible? All of this is important because it underlies the nature of the difficulty in autism.

Our own view is that there is an inbuilt disturbance in perception (which we will elaborate further below) which means that the world is somehow seen objectively, in a way that is not only devoid of social meaning but also of emotional directedness. This means that the physical properties of objects may be more salient than their functional, emotional or social significance. At the extreme, objects would only be responded to according to their ability to attract attention (through such primitive features as brightness, proximity and movement), and a sense of purposeful action, of agency, would be slow to develop. In time, for all but those with the most severe additional learning difficulties, patterns would emerge and there would be directed search for objects to fulfil repetitive actions, looking for the piece of fluff to twiddle, the angles and shadows made as fingers are held against a stream of light, the simple effect of turning a light on and off. The more able will begin to see patterns in people's behaviour and to work out cause and effect relations, but social and emotional stimuli may never give rise to intuitive insights into another (or even into themselves). They will not, then, directly perceive someone's joy or despair, although they can come to 'work out' how certain facial expressions and behaviours are associated with certain given labels such as 'sad' or 'happy', and they may even, with skilled teaching, come to recognise and respond to their own emotions and learn to apply these concepts to others. To paraphrase a very able young man with autism: 'If only someone had told me what my emotions *were*, instead of always trying to get me to control or express them!' (Sinclair, 1992).

## Experiencing the World

There is a sense in which one can both experience the world and know that one has experienced it. This latter level (the level of conscious awareness) is essential if learning is to be transferable and eventually generalisable. The learner needs to be aware of having learnt something to be able to use that knowledge flexibly in future problem solving situations. In autism, however, there seems to be a difficulty in respect of the way in which the world is experienced.

As indicated above, certainly individuals with autism experience the world, indeed they may present as experiencing acutely what is happening in terms of particular sounds, sights and so on. But there is a quality to that experiencing which suggests that while they are aware at one level that things are happening they are not aware that those things are happening *to them*. A range of phenomena in autistic thinking and behaving (e.g.

difficulties in agency, use of pronouns, remembering personal episodes) suggest that the relationship between *self* and *experience* is unique in autism. We have described elsewhere in some detail (Jordan and Powell, 1995) the role of the *experiencing self* in autism. Here it may suffice to note that what is important for the educator is an understanding that any learning experience is precisely that: an experience which the learner has and which may or may not correlate with what is presented or organised by the teacher. In short, what is delivered by the teacher is not always what is received by the pupil.

In autism then, children may perform tasks satisfactorily but they may do so in a way which remains detached from any sense of self. They may do things but not be aware at a meta level that they are doing them; they may be able to act but not reflect upon that action in such a way as to make it into a meaningful learning experience. In this way autistic learning remains at the level of the particular. Able adults with autism describe very clearly this sense of things happening as if they were witnessing a video of life, rather than being actively involved in it. The memory of those events, therefore, will not have this personal element (as will be detailed below) and all learning will become habitual and rote, being cued by the environment, by the teacher, or by the action that comes before. Rituals and routines, are not just a way of creating regularity in an otherwise confusing perceptual world, they are also ways of re-activating memory sequences and cueing their own learning.

Clearly, there are implications for the educator in all of this. First teachers need to recognise this fundamental feature of autistic thinking and try to offer alternative structures that will fulfil the functions that spontaneous reflection performs in non-autistic learning. That is, they can draw the child's attention to the salient features of a task and, more importantly, to the way in which the child him/herself is going about it. They can build in time, in every learning session, for reflection on what *the child* has experienced and learnt and how that learning relates to past learning and to future planned experiences. Second they need to use emotionally salient experiences as contexts for learning. Children with autism need to be made aware of how they are feeling about what they are doing when they are engaged in learning situations and we need to capitalise on their natural interests and involvement, rather than expect them to 'tune in' to ours. We suggest that it is the evaluative appraisal of new learning that is missing in autism and therefore that appraisal has to be made explicit so it can become the focus of any planned learning experience.

## Memory

As indicated above, a difficulty in experiencing events as personally relevant, will lead to individuals with autism being able to perform rote memory tasks satisfactorily (and sometimes extremely well) but having difficulty in remembering what they have done (without cueing), even a short while previously. For example, a boy with autism could remember considerable detail about the route taken by a particular visitor to the school, even though it was a year since her last visit, but was unable to report what he himself had been doing during the morning, when the visitor asked an open question. In this example, rote memory (aided by the child's interest in routes) is triggered by the 'prompt' of the appearance of the visitor and there is no need for any spontaneous searching of memory for information about the visitor. However, without some cue as to what the memory is, the child cannot use his sense of himself (and the memories attached to this) to search his memory as others can. He has to wait for a more specific cue, perhaps fairly general, as in 'What did you do in woodwork today?' or even needing to be very specific, 'What did you make with Mr. Smith today, using wood, which you sawed and hammered?'.

Alternatively, the boy could give the questioner 'semantic' personal memories; in other words, he could say what he usually does, or what he knows about himself (or about the context) in a general way. A teacher working with us on developing reflective approaches, for example, had a long discussion with a boy with autism about the 'lemon meringue pie' he had told her he had made in response to her query about 'What did you do in cookery today?'. It was only when she spoke to the cookery teacher later, she found that he had in fact made a shepherd's pie. In this case, the question was not specific enough to cue a personal episodic memory of what he had done in that particular cookery lesson, but instead cued a semantic memory of cookery lessons in general, picking out the ones he was most interested in because he liked lemon meringue pie.

What we are suggesting here is not that the child with autism is likely to have a poor memory for events overall, but rather a poor *personal* event memory . Because that personal dimension is missing, spontaneous search of memory for the details of an event is difficult and the child has to rely on being directly cued. Experienced teachers may well develop the 'right' level of cueing to elicit memories from children with autism, without necessarily being aware of what they are doing. This may be an effective compensatory strategy in the short term, but it may mask the child's difficulties with memory. Failures in situations where the staff are less experienced, or do not know the child as well, are then put down to problems in motivation or compliance since the teacher feels that the child 'remembers when he wants to'. That is why it is important for the teacher to analyse and reflect on his or her own behaviour, as well as that of the child, if the child is to be taught to become a more independent learner.

Ways of moving the children from dependence on cued memory towards more effective memory strategies, however, are not straightforward. The teacher needs to support the children's learning and not expose them to catastrophic failure, with no memories to rely on. Thus, it would be both cruel and pointless simply to remove the cues. The problem can be tackled on two fronts. In one, the child will be taught to self-cue and so to gain more independence in learning situations. In the other, a more remedial approach would be adopted, whereby the 'experiencing self', and through that personal event memories, would attempt to be established by emphasising the children's involvement in tasks. This could be done, using explicit means such as commenting on actions verbally or using photographs, videos or mirrors to draw the children's attention to their own role in the activity.

The notion of remediation of thinking in autism leads us to the final dimension of autistic thinking that we wish to consider, that of emotion. Any notion of remediation has to take account of the context in which experiences become salient and ones in which encoding via an experiencing self can take place.

## Emotion

While it is clear that children with autism experience emotions it is less clear that they can reflect on them or use emotion to evaluate situations and imbue them with personal meaning. Emotion has often been treated by psychologists as separate from cognition, but more recently (Iveson, 1996), it has become apparent that emotion has a dual role. Part of that role is the feeling and expression of emotion, and at least some aspects of that may be intact in autism. But it is now known that the parts of the mid brain responsible for emotional arousal, also have connections with the cortical operations of thinking and problem-solving. There is also some evidence of damage to those areas in autism (Damasio and Maurer, 1978) and this would point to difficulties in attaching any notion of personal appraisal to what is seen or thought about. Thinking would become objective rather than subjective and there would be the range of difficulties identified above in meaningful perception, personal awareness and memory.

Undoubtedly learning could still take place in a purely cognitive sense, and (unless they also have additional general learning difficulties) there is no evidence that children with autism fail to learn in any global way. Information can be learnt by rote and recalled by a mechanistic set of learnt cues. But this is not the kind of learning that can be described as 'meaningful'. Rather, it is learning which remains at the level at which it was encoded, it is not readily transferable, it is not easy to act upon or to use flexibly or creatively. For learning to be 'meaningful' it has to change to some degree the way in which the learners perceive the world or their place in the world. As we have indicated, such change requires evaluation on the part of the learner. To go beyond rote learning requires that the learner evaluate new knowledge in terms of what he/she already knows. This is not to argue that the kind of evaluative appraisal we are implying is necessarily a conscious process within non-autistic thinking. But what we do argue is that it is an essential process if meaningful learning is to take place. Without the ability to evaluatively appraise new knowledge in terms of its significance to oneself and its relatedness to what one already knows it is also difficult to establish intentionality .

This seems then to be the case in autism: the ability to use emotional states to enable personal meaning to come into being is, in some measure, impaired. Once again, the overall effect is to make it more difficult for the person with autism to 'go beyond the information given', and to pay attention to anything other than what seemingly 'grabs' the attention. It also makes one's own intentions and those of others, opaque, and so simple repetitive sequences of actions will be favoured over those involving elaborate problem-solving towards an intended goal. Memories will be in rote sequences of cues and events that are arbitrarily associated, rather than in personally meaningful narratives that give meaning, purpose and continuity to one's existence. Finally, it explains why people with autism may have strong emotions but yet be unable to use them to direct their thinking and learning.

Teaching may use the child's emotional involvement with a narrow range of activities and try to extend and share in that, rather than hoping to develop cognitive appraisal without this emotional component. There are examples of joining children in their own motivated activities in this book. Alternatively, the emotional route to learning can be by-passed by teaching personal meaning in a step by step artificial way that makes each step explicit. Examples of such a painstaking approach also appear in this book, but learning by this route is always likely to be limited. There are even approaches that attempt to do both – making the steps to personal (via interpersonal) evaluation explicit and meaningful through the use of music, which is also intended to engage the emotions.

We suggest that, by analysing teaching in autism, we will increase awareness of areas within normal development that the child with autism will be unable to access. Through our analysis it should become apparent that where non-autistic children are able to make use of affective, intuitional routes to learning, those with autism may not. The kind of spontaneous evaluative appraisal that typifies non-autistic learning is vital for meaningful learning to take place and what is needed, therefore, is either some attempt to establish this evaluative appraisal or a way of enabling those with autism to use a general cognitive route to learning. In short, explicit teaching of meaning is required for the autistic where it is not for the non-autistic; the child's attention must be drawn explicitly to how new information affects the way in which he/she understands the world. In this sense, transferability of knowledge becomes a process that needs to be directly taught rather than assumed. Children with autism need to have the links with past knowledge, and with skills to be learnt in the future, made for them at the level of instruction or made part of the experience for them as a direct product of the way in which the task is structured.

## The Interrelatedness of the Dimensions

We have argued for a view of autistic thinking and learning in which four interrelated dimensions need to be accounted for. Children with autism are not unthinking, nor are they unemotional; they do not necessarily have 'poor memories' and they do not go through life without experiencing the world. But in each of these respects they are different from the non-autistic. There is a sense in which, in all of these dimensions, they remain at a level which is operational but not reflective. In autism there is a difficulty in stepping up to a level which involves the individual in reflection upon how he/she is operating.

The question of which of the four dimensions noted in this chapter is primary to the others is perhaps the wrong question to ask. What makes autism unique is that it is precisely in the interrelatedness of the dimensions that the problem is to be found. In short, it is not that one difficulty causes another (or the others) but rather that the difficulty is in the fact that causation breaks down.

## Special Educational Needs

What we have done above is to speculate upon the nature of autism. What we need to do now is to consider the way in which autism features within individuals in terms of contributing to their special educational needs.

We have already suggested that autism in itself does not present a generalised difficulty with learning (though there may be associated learning difficulties). Yet clearly, if we have described the four dimensions at all accurately then it must be apparent that there will be subsequent difficulties in learning about the world and these will be compounded if that learning is to take place within the social setting of formal schooling. Further, for the most part we have not included in our analyses the fact that there will be varying levels of cognitive ability and language ability which will interact with the autism to present particular levels and types of special need for each individual.

Certainly, one might argue that there are things, such as the need for structured learning situations, that are common throughout the range of abilities in autism and that therefore effective teaching is a matter of finding a level at which such structure can be realised in a way which is effective for the individual child. Yet the situation is more complicated than that. For one thing the provision of structure may increase dependency if ways of increasing the student's control over that structure is not (eventually) built into the task in some way. Also, the individual's language abilities will govern the degree to which he/she can generalise the learning however well its presentation is structured. In this sense 'success' in teaching in autism may be deceptive.

Perhaps the most productive way forward at this point in this book is to consider the prospect of schooling from the perspective of individuals with autism – taking therefore the case of particular children as exemplars of the kinds of needs that arise rather than as indicators of any particular sets of such needs. In the first instance we will consider the situation of a child who has autism and a reasonably high level of intellectual functioning and who is placed in a mainstream school, and in the second that of a child with autism and associated learning difficulties who is in a specialist placement.

In the first situation the initial experience for the child is likely to be one of puzzlement. For all children the first encounter with the formal world of the school is to a greater or lesser extent 'disturbing' in as much as the accepted social order changes and new sets of demands are (socially) conveyed. For the child with autism there is the immediate difficulty of not recognising the social signals that convey the new demands. So, for him/her it is not so much learning how to cope with schooling but rather how to learn about how teachers and others in the setting go about conveying what schooling is all about. Where for the non-autistic child learning about the social world of school is largely about finding out how to make friends and get on with others, for the child with autism it is about trying to learn what friends are. So, the autistic child is, in a sense, always (or at least in most things) one dimension removed from the kind of learning that is needed by peers.

The child with autism, therefore, has a primary special need which relates to needing a curriculum that is directed specifically to the kinds of learning that he /she needs to engage in before he/she can be seen as ready for the kinds of curriculum demands that are placed immediately on non-autistic peers. Assumptions should not be made. Children with autism will need a kind of schooling which includes, as a planned part of the curriculum, teaching in those kinds of skills and aspects of knowledge that they find difficult yet which are accepted as spontaneous or 'natural' for the non-autistic. They will need to be *taught* to recognise their own emotions and those of others, to 'read' the intentions of staff when they give instructions, to interpret 'motivating' messages, to transfer knowledge from one circumstance to another, and to understand the meaning of the whole.

Having defined that a child has a special need in terms of curriculum content it is also clear that there is a subsequent special need in terms of how this newly defined content should be delivered. The fast moving, often compartmentalised, predominantly social, often implied, multi-media, delivery of new knowledge and skills, that is typical of mainstream classrooms, will not be appropriate for our child with autism. (We do not offer this scenario in any critical sense, but rather crudely summarise an approximation of what schooling in the mainstream is like, for the sake of trying to take the child's perspective). The child will have difficulty when implications rather than assertions are used, where the necessary information (to solve a problem) is not visually present throughout the task, when the purpose and meaning behind an activity is not made clear at the outset of a task and repeated for the sake of reflection at the end of the task, when transfer of previous knowledge is assumed rather than made plain. So, there are a number of special needs wrapped up here all of which need addressing if the learning experience for the child with autism is not to become a matter of the child vainly using the power of rote memory to overcome an inability to make sense of the new information at a level of personal meaning.

The second instance to be considered here is that of the child with autism and associated learning difficulties placed in a specialist setting. There will be subtle but important distinctions from our first exemplar. Here the child lacks the cognitive ability to compensate for his/her 'autistic' inability to learn in the same spontaneous, self-directed way as non-autistic peers. Such a child is less likely to be able to rely on a good rote memory ability to circumvent the usual route to learning new information and is less likely to be able to work out in a logical way the meaning of social scenarios. This child then has a need for a further restructuring of curriculum content; his/her need to learn to learn is more acute.

# References

Damasio, A.R. & Maurer, R.G. (1978) 'A neurological model for childhood autism'. *Archives of Neurology,* **35,** 777–786.

Hobson, F. P. (1993) *Autism and the Development of Mind.* London: Erlbaum.

Iveson, S. D. (1996) 'Communication in the mind'. Paper to the International Congress of Psychology XXVI Montreal. *International Journal of Psychology,* **31**, 254.

Jordan, R.R. & Powell, S.D. (1995) *Understanding and Teaching Children with Autism.* Chichester: Wiley.

Sinclair, J. (1992) 'A personal perspective', in E. Schopler and G. Mesibov (eds) *High Functioning Individuals with Autism.* New York: Plenum Press.

Wing, L. (1988) 'The continuum of autistic characteristics', in E. Schopler & G. Mesibov (Eds) *Diagnosis and Assessment in Autism.* New York: Plenum Press.

# CHAPTER 2

# Translating theory into practice

Rita Jordan and Stuart Powell

## Introduction

In the last chapter, we tried to give some indication of the practical implications of the key areas of difficulty that we suggested were at the heart of autism. In this chapter, we hope to take that further, by giving more practical details of what these difficulties might mean in the classroom and how the teacher might attempt to meet the needs of pupils with such identified difficulties. Where the last chapter focused on the specific differences found in autism that we characterised as an 'autistic' way of thinking and learning, this chapter will take more of a teacher's perspective, addressing concerns that may arise in both experienced and inexperienced teachers of pupils with autism.

Here we expand on what we mean when we talk of 'good practice', especially in relation to autism and discuss the difference between defining and recognising such practice. We go on to recognise some of the concerns of teachers of pupils with autism in a variety of settings and we suggest ways forward for the inexperienced teacher of children with autism who may be tempted to uncritical adoption of a set approach. From this, we argue that we are far from being able to identify a single approach as being the 'best' for pupils with autism and we explore the range and diversity of the special educational needs presented by pupils with autism. We then develop principles that teachers can operate in choosing a teaching approach and examine the advantages and disadvantages of an eclectic approach.

We return to the concerns of the teacher in our discussion of how measures to make schools and teachers accountable for the progress of their pupils translates into practice when considering a range of pupils with autism, in a variety of provision. We look at quality assurance measures, including both OFSTED inspections and autism-specific accreditation of services, and discuss their likely impact on the quality of teaching and learning for pupils with autism. The nature of the desirable and the possible curriculum for pupils with autism is debated and we offer a rationale for the curriculum areas covered in the remaining chapters of the book and a recognition of those that have been omitted. Finally, we end with an analysis of the challenge presented by autism and ways in which teachers and the educational system might meet that challenge.

## What is 'Good Practice' in Autism?

The issue of what constitutes 'good practice', even among teachers of normally developing mainstream pupils, is problematic. Some relate it to the kind of output measures and quality judgements that are favoured by government inspections such as OFSTED. Others see it less as a measure of excellence and more as the 'norm' of teaching, somewhat akin to a notion of a 'good enough' teacher. How does a consideration of the needs of pupils with autism affect that issue? At a recent conference, an international 'expert' in the field of autism suggested that good practice in autism could simply be equated with good practice anywhere – being what a 'good teacher' did. Is that true? Is normally defined 'good teaching' all that is required to ensure 'good practice' in autism? Well, of course it depends in part on what is meant by 'good teaching' and, on being challenged, the 'expert' conceded that her notion of a good teacher would include one who made him or herself knowledgeable about whatever medical condition the pupils suffered from, in this case, autism. This can be taken as one possible definition of 'good practice' as equalling 'that shown by a good teacher with knowledge of autism'.

Will that do? Is knowledge of autism as a medical condition sufficient to ensure good practice in working with autism in the classroom? It seems unlikely, even when dealing with normally developing children, that there would be a perfect transition between knowing about a condition and knowing how to work with individuals with the condition. It seems even less likely when thinking of autism where there will be such individual variation, where many of the strategies might involve acts that would be counter-intuitive to the 'good' teacher of non-autistic children, and where special needs are not just reflected in delays or defects in relation to 'the norm', but in a radically different way of thinking and learning.

With increased public awareness of autism and the proliferation of one day courses and seminars, many teachers are developing at least a cursory knowledge of autism and its implications. This is a positive step, if it leads to an awareness of the complexity of the condition and the recognition that there is more to be known both in terms of understanding the condition, and ways of meeting the needs that arise from it. It is less positive if, as is sometimes the case, just the difficulties are emphasised, so that the teacher is left feeling that intervention is pointless or needs to be left to 'specialists'.

One of us was once supervising a trainee-teacher student in special needs as she did her teaching practice in a school for pupils with severe learning difficulties. On the first visit, the student and the teacher showed the supervisor the class, engaged on a range of table-top activities, all except one lad who was under the table twirling a bit of cloth in his hand and rocking vigorously. There seemed to be no attempt on the part of the teacher or student to involve this pupil and so the supervisor drew their attention to the boy and asked what he was supposed to be doing, 'Oh, that's all right!' the teacher said in the tone of someone explaining things to the ignorant, 'He's got autism, and that's what they do'. It may well be what they do if left alone, but teachers need the knowledge and the support to know when and how to intervene and how to make that intervention effective.

That may be an extreme reaction, but there are still numerous examples of where teachers, especially perhaps in mainstream, either do not fully appreciate the nature and extent of the child's difficulties or are unwilling (or perhaps unable) to alter their own approach to teaching to accommodate those difficulties. Parents of children with autism are still often told by mainstream teachers, even when the child is academically able, that, if his or her problems are that severe they do not 'belong' in a mainstream school. Ironically, it may be the very wish not to separate and segregate children that leads to educationists refusing to 'label' a child or to see the value of a diagnostic category such as autism, which in turn leads to the interpretation of behaviour as wilful and the subsequent expulsion when the child fails to conform.

We would suggest, therefore, that recognition of autism as a condition with important educational consequences is a first step to creating good practice. Then there has to be some understanding of the kinds of difficulties that were outlined in the last chapter, so that behaviour is not misinterpreted and the children's difficulties and strengths in particular contexts (their special educational needs) are understood. Yet it is here that there must be an interface with 'good teaching'. Without the skills of observation, the capacity to motivate and involve, the knowledge of how to structure situations to promote learning, knowledge about autism will not translate into good practice. The art and science of teaching has to be informed by the knowledge of autism, but it also has to exist in its own right . Without it, practitioners are reduced to following set routines and recipes and some home treatment programmes are indeed based on this, so that they can be performed by para-professionals and parents. Such programmes have some value (and indeed extensive claims are made for their success), if only that they offer intensive early positive intervention, but they are also limited. 'Good practice' should involve professional judgement and the capacity to adjust the programme to meet the changing needs of the child and the situation.

The National Autistic Society in the UK, in conjunction with its affiliated societies has developed an accreditation service, whereby the autism-specific quality of services (including schools) can be assessed and the establishment or service awarded accredited status, once certain standards have been met. In relation to schools, in particular, it was felt that this accreditation process should not duplicate the OFSTED inspection of schools for quality but rather should look only at the autism specific nature of what was offered. It was also felt that, as a peer review process, it should not pre-determine the methods or approaches that any school might use to meet the needs of pupils with autism.

Neither constraint proved entirely workable in practice. It was found impossible to recommend that a school be awarded accredited status for meeting the needs of pupils with autism, if it were doing so in the overall context of teaching approaches and a curriculum that would not meet the minimum standards of a general inspection such as that of OFSTED. The curriculum might be highly specialised, but what if it were also extremely narrow? This might be justifiable for short periods to teach skills that would allow access to a wider curriculum, but the steps to that progression would have to be in place, before the school could claim to be offering an acceptable education for any child. Equally, the teaching approach might be very specific to autism, but what if it were also completely ineffective, as shown by scientific evaluations and classroom experience? This is not fanciful, in that *Facilitated Communication* might be said to be relatively autism-specific (although it was developed for children with different needs and translates the needs of those with autism to fit the population for whom it was designed i.e. it claims that autism is a form of cerebral palsy rather than a communication disorder) and it has been shown to be ineffective in scientific evaluations. Nor has there ever been any evidence of classroom efficacy (once the cueing and prompting of the facilitator is removed). Yet there have been schools and centres where this is the only educational approach offered to pupils with autism. Aspects of Facilitated Communication (or any similar approach) might have a place within a specialist curriculum, but it is doubtful if its sole use as a teaching strategy could constitute good practice in autism.

At this stage, some of those involved in developing the process of accreditation began to have doubts about its validity on the grounds that 'good practice' could not be defined. Indeed, early attempts to reduce the task of the peer reviewers to the ticking of checklists of certain behaviours, did prove abortive as these quantitative assessments seemed to bear little relation to perceived quality. What they did do, however, is highlight the fact that professional and experienced judgements are just that, and their subjective basis cannot be disguised by attempts to provide quantitative ticklists. The objectivity must reside in the selection and training of those making the judgements and the value of the judgements resides in the quality of those making them. In effect, while it may not be possible to *define* 'good practice', it is possible to *recognise* it and it is the experience and knowledge of the observers that determines the validity of that recognition.

## The Lure of the Recipe

We have already mentioned the dangers that may arise from knowledge of autism that stops with a knowledge of the characteristic difficulties and we have shown that good practice must incorporate both knowledge of autism and good teaching techniques. We would like to mention here another source of danger in the way that some teachers and some authorities adopt training in one particular approach as *the* training in autism. The particular training packages that are marketed in this way are of variable quality, but our worries do not stem from the adoption of any particular approach, but from the notion that training in any one method will be adequate for developing expertise in working with people with autism.

It is easy to see the appeal of such courses for teachers with little experience of the condition and for authorities who are starting to make provision for pupils with autism for the first time. Certainly, approaches such as TEACCH (Schopler and Olley,1982) do offer a good starting point in that they take account of many of the difficulties shown by people with autism and they provide practical techniques and strategies that will be useful for working with most individuals with autism in most settings. The danger comes when, rather than being seen as a stepping stone towards understanding autism and the development of a full curriculum, such approaches are seen as the end point, as 'the answer'. An inspector of schools in an area of the UK recently described the bewilderment of his local authority when a specialist unit for pupils with autism was found to 'know a lot about TEACCH, but not much about autism'. For them, the two had become synonymous and they did not understand how a single approach, followed rigidly as a kind of recipe, can actually obscure greater understanding of the condition.

Peeters (in press) describes the TEACCH approach he uses in his practical training programmes in Europe and beyond, as being one of 'visually mediated instruction' and this seems to us to describe accurately what is on offer in such a programme. It offers ways of structuring the curriculum and the environment to reduce stress and to promote cued learning. It will do much for the majority of pupils with autism who need that kind of structure, at least in their early years, but it can never go beyond that structure to give the child internally cued strategies and so enable remediation of thinking and independence from the structure. Many people using this approach believe that it is a genuinely prosthetic device for people with autism, enabling them to function within their disabilities, just as a white stick may help the mobility of the blind without ever improving sight. Such a view means that, just as one would not remove a white stick once someone has learnt to function happily with it, so one would not want to remove the enabling visual structure used in TEACCH. This view is supported by examples of situations where the structure has been removed (because the child has moved, or the TEACCH trained teacher has left) and the child has immediately reverted to the levels of stress and difficult behaviour that existed before the introduction of TEACCH.

This may be a valid position for the life-long service offered by the TEACCH programme in its North Carolina base, but it does not reflect the situation for people with autism in the UK nor the aims of most schools, which would include the fostering of independent and autonomous functioning. Of course, it can increase independence from other people and aspects of the TEACCH approach can be made transportable so that children can learn to carry their own 'structure' with them into new situations (truly like the white stick of the blind). Yet this should be recognised as training rather than education; it may be useful training and for some pupils with very severe additional learning difficulties, it may be the best that can be done. But true education does need to attend to clichés such as 'developing the full potential of the child'; that is why they are clichés. All of the contributors to this book use structure in some form or another and most would acknowledge their debt to the TEACCH approach in many aspects of classroom management and in developing communicative understanding in the children. Yet all have developed towards a more cognitive approach that seeks to give as much responsibility, for their own learning, as possible, back to the child.

## Principles and Eclecticism

Thus, we would want to eschew adherence to any one approach, especially when followed as a set recipe. We recognise that teachers would sometimes wish to know exactly what to do with Johnnie on Monday morning, but we also know that most teachers recognise this as an unsatisfactory solution to their difficulties. An outsider may be able to offer something useful to resolve a particular situation with a particular child (and there will be times when all of us get stuck in our approach to a problem and it helps to talk it over with others and gain fresh insights and suggestions) but most teachers do not want the sense of being de-skilled, which comes from having to follow someone else's package without being able to adapt it or extend it. In our experience, what teachers want is to know what strategies are available and to understand both the potentialities and the limitations of their use. They want the time and the resources to enable them to observe and make their own evaluations of the child and the situation, and they want sufficient flexibility within their work situations to enable them to apply the strategies and approaches their professional judgement dictates.

Many teachers, then, describe the approach they use as 'eclectic' and will go on to elaborate to the effect that they 'take the best from a range of different approaches'. This could represent, as the teachers suggest, the best of all worlds, or it could be chaotic with the benefits of one approach being negated or unrealised because another approach has a directly contrary effect. It may also mean that no one approach is given a chance and that the teacher does not really understand the rationale for each approach, but only uses some technique that has a different meaning and value divorced from its proper context.

Take, for example, a situation where the teacher is using the Option approach (Kaufman, 1994) to develop interpersonal interaction for a period or two in the week. The essence of this approach is that the child is fully in control of the interaction, the adult follows the child's lead and, although the child is invited to join in extended activities by the adult with 'energy, enthusiasm and excitement', the adult always accepts if the child refuses and the child is never forced either to stop or to undertake any action. Let us say, further, that the school also uses intensive behaviour modification techniques, such as those that form part of the programme used by Lovaas and his colleagues (McEachin et al., 1993) to build early functional and academic skills. This is a highly adult-controlled programme with pre-determined targets which are rewarded with external reinforcers (such as spoonfuls of jam), prompting to engage in set tasks and punishment (in more recent versions restricted to a sharp 'No') for mistakes or non-compliance.

The rationale for Option is that putting the child in control of interactions with adults, plus the way in which the adult imitates the child's actions, should make adults more predictable and less disturbing and thus enable the child to make more approaches and to retreat less into stereotyped behaviour. The rationale for Lovaas style interventions is that the child will learn through positive reinforcement of correct responses and an important part of this will be that there is only one 'correct' response in each situation. As can be seen, from the child's perspective, the two situations represent directly opposed learning experiences. On the one hand, they are being encouraged to make spontaneous moves towards interactive play with an adult and to enjoy rather than fear the experience. On the other, they are being made to conform in a very set way, there is stress in having to identify and produce the one correct response on cue and the adult may dispense spoonfuls of jam but may also dispense sharp reprimands which may even be shouted (from witnessing some Lovaas style programmes). It may seem as if we are suggesting that one of these approaches is better than the other; it is true that Option is more easily accommodated within our approach than Lovaas, but that is not the point we are trying to make. The point is, that to employ both approaches would be confusing and the aims of neither programme are likely to be fulfilled.

Even where the elements from different approaches that are used do not contradict one another, there may be problems in an eclectic approach. A curriculum is of its essence a matter of priorities and choices. When there is so much for pupils with autism to learn beyond, as well as within, the traditional curriculum framework (as might be characterised by National Curriculum subjects), teaching one thing, or in one way, must mean that the teacher is failing to teach something else or in another way. It is not only important, therefore, that what is done fits together in a coherent whole and that each part of the curriculum contributes to the overall aims for the child, but also that there is a principled rationale for teaching one thing rather than another or in one way rather than another. These principles should reflect what is known of autism, what is known of the child and the overall educational philosophy of the school (such as 'promoting independence and personal autonomy'). They should respect, and incorporate where possible, the views of the parents and of the child. This may involve elements that come originally from an eclectic trawl of different approaches, but the dangers of this are avoided by the principles guiding their inclusion and the way in which they fit together to serve the overall educational aims for that child.

## Accountability and Rationale

We have already mentioned the role of OFSTED inspections and the National Curriculum and both these facts of life in the UK will have effects on what is offered to pupils with autism, as they do for all children. The two areas are related in that one of the factors influencing the extent to which the National Curriculum is followed in the curriculum for pupils with autism, is the knowledge that adherence to it (unless it, or a part of it, has been specifically disapplied for any child) will form part of the grounds for inspection. Yet we would not want to suggest that the only reason for following the National Curriculum with pupils with autism was this fear of accountability from inspections. We discuss the pros and cons of the

National Curriculum below, but our evidence is that more OFSTED inspectors are now open to variations in the National Curriculum framework, providing there is still due regard for that framework, the curriculum offered is broad and balanced and there is a clear rationale for the curriculum offered. However, there is great individual variation between OFSTED teams and there may also be greater expectations of following the National Curriculum in mainstream schools, for example, than in specialist schools for those with autism.

Of more concern, in relation to OFSTED inspections, is the nature of their understanding of what constitutes 'good practice' in autism and how this affects the judgements made about schools and teachers. A working party from the Association of Heads and Teachers of Adults and Children with Autism (AHTACA, unpublished) produced a document commenting on the guidelines given to OFSTED inspectors and suggesting amendments and cautionary notes in relation to pupils with autism. This was accepted, but there has been no evidence of its effect on practice and nor is its content reflected in the amended guidelines that have since been published. We know personally of schools for pupils with autism who have found the OFSTED inspection a positive experience and felt that it was helpful rather than inhibitory of good practice. But, equally, we have heard of horror stories where, for example, a teacher was castigated for too low expectations in the encouragement of expressive speech when the session was meant to teach choice and the child was being encouraged to use 'yes' and 'no' appropriately for this purpose (rather than a child who was capable of 3-word phrases only being encouraged to use single words, which was the interpretation of the lesson by the OFSTED inspectors). The difference between the two kinds of experience seems to depend to a large extent on the knowledge and understanding of autism in the particular OFSTED team, but schools should prepare for ignorance and make the rationale for both curriculum choice and the objectives of specific lessons very explicit.

As indicated above, the National Curriculum is also somewhat problematic when it comes to autism. There is nothing within it that of itself would necessarily be irrelevant to pupils with autism and we would not argue for disapplication on the grounds of autism alone. Indeed, one of us was involved in the early days of the introduction of the National Curriculum, in developing ways of providing access to it for pupils with autism (Jordan, 1991). The problem rests with the issues raised in the section above about the time constraints and the priority choices. There is so much that needs to be taught to pupils with autism that lies outside of the National Curriculum (early interaction and communication skills, flexible problem solving and so on) that may overshadow the merits of history or geography, for example. Of course, there are inventive and creative ways of using the National

Curriculum subjects to teach the really vital skills needed in autism, but many teachers resent the time taken in such 'creative accountancy' or 'tokenism' when there is so much else that needs to be done.

The arguments will depend on the setting to some extent and teachers will have more freedom to be flexible in specialist settings than in those where there is an expectation of integration with mainstream peers either currently or in the future. Part of the problem with specialist provision, may be that too specialised a curriculum is allowed to develop and so future opportunities for integration are curtailed, not because they would not meet the needs of the child, but because the original segregation has been reinforced by a specialised curriculum which has effectively denied access to the one followed in mainstream settings. Yet the arguments for the National Curriculum on the grounds of inclusion are not very convincing. It was not originally designed with all children (including those with autism) in mind, so it cannot be considered to be an inclusive curriculum.

Practical difficulties within the National Curriculum lie in the way that skill hierarchies are assumed in the acquisition of knowledge and skills, which does not necessarily accord with the developmental pattern in autism. There are additional problems in the way that much of the learning is encouraged to be social and in the way that the most vital area of the curriculum for individuals with autism – personal and social education (PSE) – is marginalised. In adapting the National Curriculum teachers need to look at ways of emphasising PSE across the curriculum and to provide assessment in these areas so that progress can be monitored. There is also a need to separate clearly those skills needed in academic life and those appropriate to 'real' life, since the child with autism will not make the distinction and may not have acquired basic social skills in the home context before coming to school; this is particularly important for communication. 'Integrated' children in particular will need to learn about classroom discourse styles but they must have these clearly distinguished from everyday communication skills, which will also need to be taught directly. The aim must be not to fit pupils into the National Curriculum but to see what aspects of the latter can be used to meet their needs. The first and most important aspect of entitlement is entitlement to a curriculum suitable to meet the needs of the individual for personal and academic growth. Special skills should not be seen as a problem but as a resource for the further education of that individual.

## A Curriculum for Autism

A curriculum for pupils with autism, therefore, may or may not incorporate the National Curriculum, but it should have the following features. Its content should be determined by the needs of the child, rather than cultural values in respect to academic subjects and so it needs to be pupil centred and not subject centred. It will need to give priority to communication and interpersonal areas include the specific teaching of cultural norms and meanings. Functional and life skills should be involved from the start (there is no reason why the child should not be sorting knives from forks, or socks from pants, rather than plastic bunnies from plastic Christmas trees), although we would be wary of having too low expectations and teaching children of 12 to clean toilets (as happens in some curricula) on the grounds that they will be expert by the time they are ready to take a job.

We would also take an eclectic leaf from the Higashi approach (Quill et al., 1989), as well as from British primary school survival tactics, and include a period each day of sustained physical activity. There is some danger of this becoming addictive, but it is a relatively healthy addiction and there is other evidence of the beneficial effects in terms of stress reduction for the pupils (and staff) and the consequent lessening of disruptive and challenging behaviours. All centres should look at ways of encouraging integration and teaching the child with autism skills that will help to make this successful. This applies whether or not the child is already in a mainstream setting (where it will help to ensure that integration is a process and not just a location) or whether he or she is in a specialist setting with scant prospect of immediate integration, since there will need to be education for integration into the community and reverse integration (where mainstream pupils go into the specialist setting) should be at least a possibility. Thus, there will need to be training in imitation and observational skills, and then a way of providing access to normally developing peers to practise the skills and to have them prompted and drawn to the child's attention in real life contexts.

As we have indicated earlier, we would not advocate any single teaching approach, but, whatever is chosen should involve the following. There needs to be some form of structure to minimise stress and promote learning and, in most cases, this is most appropriately provided through visual structure, as in the TEACCH programme. Children with additional visual problems will be a clear, if rare, exception to this, and for them the structure will need to be through tactile or, less successfully, through audition. In accordance with our own views on the fundamental difficulties in autism, the teaching approach should be one that provides opportunities for learning to learn. This will involve addressing each of the areas of difficulty identified in the last chapter and providing direct teaching in areas where intuitive understanding is lacking.

Most children with autism will need some access to 1:1 teaching, although there are some who cannot tolerate this kind of confrontational contact (especially if the teacher sits across the table from the child) and will respond better in small groups. Note that we advocate merely access to 1:1 teaching so that in some cases the time allocation can be used by the teacher to observe rather than teach. Although children with autism will have particular difficulties in learning in and from groups, this does not mean that they should be shielded entirely from group teaching. As is shown in Golding Chapter 4, in this volume, groups have much to offer the child with autism. Difficulties need to be seen as a challenge and an opportunity, rather than an indication that this aspect of curriculum work should be denied.

As discussed earlier, it is important that schooling for children with autism does not become a succession of activities devised to address their difficulties; their strengths also need to be developed and encouraged so that we can maximise potential in all areas of development. In the same way, the difficulties should not be a barrier to experiences, but rather the teacher should ask of a desired goal 'What support will this child need in order to participate in this activity? What skills?' and then set about trying to provide them. One of the saddest situations known to the authors was a teenager in a mainstream comprehensive school who had Asperger's Syndrome. His great love was computer studies, but he was forbidden to attend the computer club at lunchtimes because he needed to attend remedial English lessons. Of course teachers do need to address weaknesses but they should remember the child's overall experience of school and try to think of ways of addressing weaknesses through strengths. Murray (Chapter 7) gives a moving example of doing just that with a young man with autism.

As well as in its content and teaching approach, the curriculum for pupils with autism needs to be specialised in its organisation and the environment in which it takes place. Teachers should try to engender an atmosphere of trust and high expectations, with the trust including an understanding of the child's real difficulties rather than a misperception of them as resulting from laziness or aggression, or whatever. Parents are important as partners throughout education, but this is even more the case in autism where there needs to be consistency across all settings if the child is to progress, and where communicative and early interactive skills are often best fostered in a home setting. In line with our earlier arguments on the importance of teachers knowing about autism and the kinds of differences in thinking and learning that can be expected as a result, the curriculum should include policies of staff development in understanding autism.

Finally, we would make a plea for education, not containment or training. We have already stressed how much there is for the pupil with autism to learn and how dependent such pupils are on being taught explicitly. They cannot afford to spend time on occupation tasks, unless there is a specific educational goal of teaching the child to perform the task in a social group, or independently or faster than before. We have sometimes seen classes arranged and resourced so that the child has 1:1 time with an adult, only to find that it is wasted by the adult not quite knowing how to use this time. The teacher may get the child to perform a task they can already do (mere occupation) or may interfere with the child's spontaneous behaviour, not to extend the play or teach a new procedure, but seemingly because this is the time allotted for 1:1 work. Teaching 1:1 should not be assumed to be like group teaching, only easier; it is not! Teachers will need training themselves on how to observe and interpret what the child is doing and, as we point out later in the book, when to intervene and when to hold back.

None of it is easy, but it is rewarding, especially if we sometimes manage to 'get it right'. Later chapters show instances of how skilled practitioners have managed to 'get it right' at least some of the time, although we are sure that they would be the first to admit that that is not always the case. No one has all the answers or even *an* answer, least of all us. But we do feel we can recognise and applaud good practice when we see it.

# References

AHTACA (unpublished) *Guidelines for OFSTED on the Inspection of Schools Catering for Pupils within the Autistic Spectrum*. London: AHTACA.

Jordan, R. R. (1991) *The National Curriculum: Access for Pupils with Autism*. London: Inge Wakehurst Trust/ NAS.

Kaufman, B.N. (1994) *Son Rise: the Miracle Continues*. Tiburon, CA: H.J.Kramer Inc.

McEachin, J.J., Smith, T. & Lovaas, O.I. (1993) 'Long-term outcome for children with autism who received early intensive behavioral treatment', *American Journal of Mental Retardation*, **97**, 359–372.

Peeters, T. (in press) *Working with Autism: Theory into Practice*. London: Whurr Publications.

Quill, K., Gurry, S. & Larkin, A. (1989) Daily life therapy: a Japanese model for educating children with autism. *Journal of Autism and Developmental Disorders*, **19**, 625–635.

Schopler, E. & Olley, J.G. (1982) 'Comprehensive educational services for autistic children: the TEACCH model', in C.R. Reynolds & T.R. Gutkin (eds) *Handbook of School Psychology*. New York: Wiley.

CHAPTER 3

# Developing and using play in the curriculum

Rita Jordan and Sarah Libby

## Introduction

Play is a diverse and complex behaviour that is viewed as central to the normal development of children (Bornstein and O'Reilly, 1993; Fein, 1981). In this chapter we discuss the status of play behaviours in autism and the means of developing play in a classroom setting with this group. Different forms of play behaviour will be introduced before considering the difficulties that individuals with autism have in the arena of play. Finally, some examples are given of good practice in the development of play in autism and the use of play within the curriculum.

There are at least three ways in which play is valuable in the curriculum of children with autism. First, if symbolic play can be taught, it may aid conceptual and cognitive ability, as well as improving opportunities for social engagement with others. Second, play activities can be used to engage the child emotionally and foster receptiveness to interpersonal development. Third, play can prevent secondary disabilities by enabling participation in social and cultural events (such as shared routines and the building of narrative structures), even when the child may only be following the form of the behaviour, rather than showing an understanding of its symbolic nature.

## Play and its Development

Defining play behaviours has proved to be a source of contention (see Fein, 1981 for a review). Part of the difficulty relates to the diversity of this behaviour, engaging in peek-a-boo with a six month old infant and playing firemen with a nursery age child are both play, yet it is sometimes difficult to see their common characteristics. Furthermore, these behaviours intuitively appear to have certain qualitative attributes which have been difficult to describe in scientific terms. What is clear is that, although it has often been contrasted with more serious pursuits such as 'work', play is not trivial in its effects on development.

Play develops along crucial dimensions that parallel the development of the child. In cognitive terms, play develops from sensory exploration of objects, through simple repetitive actions to purposeful problem solving, with an awareness of the functional as well as the physical properties of objects. Socially, play develops from isolated exploration of the self acting as an agent on the world, to complex, co-operative and competitive social dramas with peers. Emotionally, play develops from mutual arousal with a caregiver in joint routines, to exploration of emotional reactions to novel or created situations. Finally, play develops from a means of encoding social/cultural forms (Bruner, 1983) to ways of developing narrative structures with others and expressing them through action dramas and stories.

Thus, play both develops in itself and is essential to other development. It is not the obverse of work; it *is* the work of children, who must discover the world through activity on it with others. Disturbance of play in autism, then, leads directly to disturbance in all aspects of development. Whether this is secondary to the original 'autistic' disturbance, or is the essence of that disturbance, is uncertain. In either case, the hope is that early intervention can prevent or ameliorate some of the disturbances that arise from a failure to engage in play.

Play, then, might be characterised as incorporating *intention* (it involves an agent acting on the world), *interrelatedness* (it involves a developing interest in, and incorporation of, the other's perspective), *emotional directedness* (the play activity of its essence is interesting and involving, and engaged in for its own sake) and *narrative ability* (the play act has a characteristic narrative form). It is when we see how these abilities are disturbed in autism, we also see how interventions can address this area most effectively.

Developmentally, play begins when a caregiver and infant become engaged in simple lap play early in life. Games such as peek-a-boo, tickling and games with an element of surprise are observed in interactions with babies. These games have been described as proto-conversations (Bateson, 1975) and may act as the format for later communicative skills by introducing the child to principles such as turn-taking and narrative form (Bruner and Feldman, 1993).

Pretend play begins to emerge from twelve months, initially in the form of functional play (Leslie, 1987). Functional play has been described by Leslie as the ability to treat an object as it's function denotes even if it is a miniaturised version of this object; a child may push a car along the ground making a 'brmm' noise or feed a doll with a toy bottle. Symbolic play begins at 20 months; here children show the capacity to treat objects or situations as if they are something else. Examples of this behaviour include pretending that a brick is some soap and washing teddy, or eating invisible food. Many theorists believe that the emergence of symbolic play heralds a more global change in the infant's representational abilities (Leslie, 1987; Perner, 1991). This representational change has been linked to the development of a theory of mind; this is the ability to understand mental states that are held by oneself and others and to make inferences from them (Baron-Cohen, 1987; Leslie, 1987). Others have seen it as a necessary pre-cursor to language development (Cooper et al., 1978) and the two aspects may indeed connect through the understanding of mental state terms that are facilitated through social play routines (Dunn, 1988). Pretend play has also been related to the development of humour (McGhee, 1983).

## Play Abilities in Children with Autism

In discussions of the play abilities of those with autism, the lack of imaginative pretend play has dominated (e.g., Jarrold et al., 1993; Wing et al., 1977; Wulff, 1985). In reality, the play abilities of this group can be affected at all the levels discussed above. Although data on their early social development is problematic, due to the late diagnosis, analysis of videotapes of early interactions suggests that children with autism tend not to become involved in early lap play, and show little interest in games like peek-a-boo (Hobson, 1993). Hobson relates these difficulties to problems in developing relationships with others. However, more forceful interactions may develop these interpersonal connections and parents and teachers often report that this group can be motivated by rough and tumble and that this may promote social skills that are not apparent in other situations (Newson, 1996). Similarly, as noted below, closer structuring of the play situation may have the same effect (Christie et al., 1992; Nind and Hewett, 1994; Wimpory et al., 1995)

Experimental studies of play abilities in children with autism indicate that sensorimotor play dominates in this group beyond the verbal mental age when it declines in non-autistic infants (Libby et al., 1995; Tilton and Ottinger, 1964). Some researchers have suggested that those with autism may explore the world in a deviant manner and this may affect later abilities to engage in pretend play (Roeyers and van Berkalaer-Onnes, 1994). This may arise from the dominance of sensorimotor behaviour interfering with the normal emergence of curiosity or possible perceptual abnormalities in this group (e.g. Happé, 1995; Williams, 1996) or it may result from a failure to develop agency (Russell, 1994) or a sense of an experiencing self (Powell and Jordan, 1993).

The most widely researched play deficit is the problem encountered in pretend play. 'Pretend play' is a term used for both functional and symbolic play, although not all authors or researchers make this distinction. The nature and extent of the difficulty in pretend play in autism is far from clear (see Jarrold et al., 1993 for a review). It is well established that individuals with autism have a deficit in the production of spontaneous symbolic play (e.g. Baron-Cohen, 1987; Ungerer and Sigman, 1981) which is rarely observed in children with autism and, when it is demonstrated, it tends to be rigid and stereotyped in nature (Atlas, 1990). Some researchers have found that this deficit is not apparent in structured circumstances (Lewis and Boucher, 1988; Whyte and Owens, 1989), while others have found that the deficit remains (Riguet et al., 1981; Sigman and Ungerer, 1984). Moreover, there is continued debate on the status of functional play in this group. Some authors report a deficit (Lewis and Boucher, 1988, Jarrold et al., 1996; Sigman and Ungerer, 1984), while others claim that there are no difficulties with functional play (e.g. Baron-Cohen, 1987). Pretend play, then, is not simply absent in the autistic population and each individual child may show play behaviours that reflect not just their autism, but their history (whether they have been in contact with 'normal' play through siblings or an appropriate peer group, the teaching they have had) and the current situation (the amount of structure supporting the play required).

## Developing Play Abilities in Individuals with Autism

If the capacity to play claims such a central role in normal development it is imperative that it is addressed when working with individuals that have failed to develop these skills. First we will consider possible means of encouraging play abilities that are poorly developed.

## Lap Play

The problems observed in engaging young children with autism in lap play could relate to the difficulties in communication and social interaction observed in this group. Subtle changes in interaction style with those with autism may recreate this early form of interaction. For example, a teacher may use accentuation, dramatic pauses and explicit turn-taking to engage the child. A well-developed example of this is the use of music interaction or music supported communication which is an approach that has been developed at Sutherland House School in Nottingham (Christie et al., 1992; Prevezer, 1990; Wimpory et al., 1995). Here, live music is used to emphasise and make predictable the interactive moves between the child and the caregiver or teacher. The music will pick up on the rhythm of the child's actions and lead them to a climax with a musical coda. The type of exchanges, accompanied by appropriate music, range from imitation of the child, a commentary of their behaviour, building on spontaneous behaviours and using pauses to encourage anticipation (Newson, 1996).

Musical interaction therapy is based on observations of early interactions and the central requisite of social timing and social empathy (Newson, 1979). Very early in normal development the infant begins to negotiate interactions with their caregivers (Shotter and Newson, 1974). It has been suggested that individuals with autism have difficulty in developing these skills (Hobson, 1993). This therapy provides a means of encouraging social skills through developing an accentuated dialogue with the autistic individual that emulates the type of interactions observed between infants and caregivers. It is based on an understanding of the interactions observed between infants and adults, the developmental significance of these exchanges, and the difficulties encountered in the development of these behaviours in individuals with autism. There is no definitive evaluative research, but it was one of the approaches evaluated by Jones and Newson (1992) and was associated with good developmental outcomes in the children studied. Likewise, a case study of an individual using this approach with her mother over a period of eighteen months showed very positive results (Wimpory et al., 1995).

In the work that has been done with this approach in schools or clinical sessions the music is supplied by a third person (often a speech and language therapist who has musical ability) but in less well resourced situations parents may replace the use of musical instruments with singing and, in that case, the adult interacting with the child can supply the musical support also. This has the disadvantage in that there is not an objective third person looking at the interaction and deciding which actions of the child should be emphasised in order to develop the interaction. However, the singing adult (providing the result is musical enough to be tolerated by the child) has the advantage of not needing special skills, equipment, space or time, so that the singing can be incorporated into the daily routines of the child and it also locates the more meaningful 'music' within the interacting adult, which may make that adult a more interesting figure for the child.

In many schools, speech and language therapists have modified the original structures of music supported communication to provide group or class sessions in which these same principles are applied. In such cases there may be singing or musical games involving closure which help structure the interactions between a child and an adult, two children or even a group of children. Music is usually helpful to children with autism in that it seems to add both interest and meaning to social situations where they would otherwise be lacking. However, there is no research evidence yet about the importance of the music in this technique. It may be that the music's main function is to structure the interaction of the adult, rather than the child, so that it is slowed, repetitive and structured, in a way that normal interactions are not. On a practical level, unmusical practitioners have attempted to engage the child in similar slowed, emphasised routines without singing or using a musical instrument. This has not been evaluated, but it would be an alternative approach to try if the teaching adult is certain they could not sing. A further alternative would be to use one of the strategies given below.

Another strategy used in these early interactions is imitating and building on the behaviour of the child (Meltzoff and Gopnik, 1993). This technique has been capitalised on to encourage a range of skills in individuals with autism including social skills (Dawson and McKissick, 1984) and exploratory behaviour (Tiegerman and Primavera, 1981). A therapeutic method which uses imitation to encourage all aspects of the child's development is the Option approach (Kaufman, 1976; 1994). However, there is not adequate evaluation of the efficacy of this approach or how important imitating the child is (Jordan, 1990) as compared to other features of the programme such as its intensity. Although many parents in the UK continue to use the Option approach in home-based programmes, there are only a few schools who have incorporated Option-type sessions within their curriculum. At face value, the Option approach should increase social responsiveness, involvement with others and exploration of the world, at least within a 'safe' environment. One of the authors has seen such development within home-based programmes, although there is some doubt about how well the Option principles are carried through in such situations (Jordan and Powell, in press). How far it is possible to generalise this development beyond this extreme child-centred environment is an unresolved issue.

Imitation is also a strong feature of the interactive curriculum developed by Nind and Hewett (1994). These authors have developed their techniques for those with profound and multiple learning difficulties, who are also non-communicative and lacking in interpersonal skills and motivation. Imitating the behaviour of a child may have many limitations in terms of teaching cognitive skills, but it may be vital in developing social relations with others through which other cognitive skills may be acquired.

## Exploration

One of the central problems in this group is a tendency to perseverate on a single activity, i.e. repeat the same thing over and over again. This would also be true of other children, with severe learning difficulties for example, but autism is notable for the way in which this perseverative behaviour is shown across the ability range. Perseveration limits the child's experience and may restrict the development of flexibility and constrain exploration and play. Watson (1985) has argued that one means of developing flexibility is through changing one element of a task at a time, thus retaining some predictability while allowing limited flexibility. This principle underlies much of the TEACCH programme but can also be applied to play. For example, if a child perseverates on pushing a specific car back and forwards one may start by encouraging the child to use different vehicles, later make different movements with the vehicles and when the child can cope with this introduce other appropriate toys and incorporate these into the play e.g. a garage.

This example demonstrates another technique that may be useful. Rather than suppressing or limiting obsessions, teachers attempt to slowly build on them to encourage playful behaviour. It is not always easy to move the child on from their obsessional behaviour, but is likely be met with more interest than using a toy in which the child shows no interest. Again, this careful extension of the child's focus of interest is a feature of the Option programme (Kaufman, 1976, 1994). Where it is impossible to think of adequate ways of extending a child's obsessional behaviour, however, it may still be possible to develop other activities by using the interest as a reward for these activities. The problem is that removal of the activity after the reward period can lead to negative experiences which punish rather than reward. Teachers often solve this dilemma by offering the child a photograph of the 'reward' activity, to replace the actual activity, which can then be placed in the child's visual timetable to show the child just what has to be done before the reward activity once more becomes available. This is to adopt the approach that is used in TEACCH and other systems (Howlin and Rutter, 1978) to develop work behaviours, and to apply it to the development of other play behaviours which, as we have argued above, is 'work ' for the child.

Other studies have used similar behaviour modification techniques to reduce the amount of sensorimotor behaviour produced by these children in an attempt to encourage more appropriate play behaviours (Koegel et al., 1974). It does not follow, of course, that suppressing sensorimotor behaviour would directly encourage appropriate play to emerge. However, some use of behaviour modification techniques to differentially reinforce novel or creative, as opposed to stereotyped, play behaviours may be useful, if applied when inappropriate behaviours are felt to be dramatically restricting play development. Positively reinforcing behaviours that approximate more appropriate play may help initiate some change but teachers usually find such changes to be slow and limited to situations where the external reward is available. Nevertheless, playing games where a favourite toy is hidden and requires increasingly complex moves to retrieve (unlocking boxes in which it has been placed, listening to the directions of others in a 'hunt the thimble' type game, for example) may improve the skills necessary for exploratory play, leaving the motivation to be worked on separately.

Some places have used a version of a game used by a school and research centre in Budapest (Balazs et al., 1996) to encourage creative and social skills in relation to objects. In this version an object or, more usually, a set of objects, which offers a number of possibilities for play, is placed in front of the group. Each child in turn has to come and do something with the object(s) and must not repeat what others have done. Naturally, this is difficult for children with autism and they will need, at first, to be introduced in very small groups (two or three children at most) and there may need to be photographs also depicting the range of ways in which the object can be used in play. In time, other children can be introduced and the photographs removed, although children with additional severe learning difficulties may always need some kind of visual clue to the range of behaviours that are possible, if they are to play this game successfully.

## Social Interactions During Play

Some studies have used peers and siblings to improve play interactions, either by providing the child with autism with strategies for approaching another child or helping the normally developing child find ways to engage the child with autism (e.g. Belchic and Harris, 1994; Coe et al., 1991; Haring and Lovinger, 1989; Wooten and Mesibov, 1986). These studies report increased interactions after training. The difficulty lies in the interpretation of these changes. Is the child with autism learning to make more social interactions or just to respond to the increased social demands of others? Despite these limitations encouraging play with non-autistic peers may have many positive effects. In classrooms, Roeyers (1995) has shown that other children need only be informed about autism, rather than actually trained in how to play with children with autism, in order for there to be successful play between the groups. The further advantage found in this study was that the children with autism were then able to play more effectively with other children who had not been part of the original study. Roeyers suggests that this is because the 'untrained' (but informed) peers did not adjust their normal play routines as much as those who receive specific training in what to do when playing with children with autism. Thus, it was then easier for the children with autism to adapt to the completely unadapted play of other children.

Experience with a range of integrated settings in the UK suggests that just placing children together does not automatically result in improved play behaviour in the children with autism (e.g. Jordan and Powell, 1994). Yet varieties of informing or modified training of peers can be very successful. In many mainstream schools, where there is a unit for pupils with autism, a form of a 'buddy' system is used, both to increase the integrated play of pupils with autism and to avoid teasing and other difficulties at social 'play' times. Such schemes not only benefit the pupils with autism but are reported by teachers to develop the social and empathetic skills of the normally developing children.

Other schools and units for pupils with autism use 'reverse integration' either instead of, or as a precursor to, integration of the children with autism into mainstream settings. 'Reverse' integration, as its name implies, involves children from the mainstream setting coming into the specialised setting to play with the children with autism. This has the advantage for the children with autism that they are on their own 'home' territory and so only have to adjust to the new peers, and not to a new setting at the same time. There are reports of the success of mixed groups involving reverse integration allied to exciting activities which are attractive to the non-autistic peers.

Some schools in the UK have adopted this principle, especially in the development of out of school clubs and activities. This is often accompanied by the pre-training of the children with autism so that they already have the necessary skills to participate in the activity and can concentrate on the social skills necessary to do the activity in a group situation. A good example of this is the careful structured programme of skating skills in a school for children with severe learning difficulties in Scotland, that has specialised in provision for pupils with autism (Jordan, 1996). Children progress through Fisher-Price skates, roller skates and finally roller blades and also progress in kinds of surface and in the activities they accomplish on the skates. When they have the skills necessary for roller blade hockey, they are able to participate with siblings in after school games, to the benefit and enjoyment of all, including the parents who have a night off.

## Pretend Play

Specific training programmes in pretend play skills have used a variety of techniques. Some have used behaviour modification techniques to try and encourage pretend play, with some success (Stahmer and Schreibman, 1992; Stahmer, 1995; Thorp et al., 1995). An issue arising from this approach is the degree to which the children are developing 'learned' behaviours rather than demonstrating spontaneous play behaviours after the training. Furthermore, such approaches do not make pretend play intrinsically appealing; children may perform pretend play acts just to receive a reward without realising the meaning of their action. This can be useful as a first step in getting the children involved in social situations so that social meanings can become salient as Park (1986) showed in training her daughter to respond to social greetings by allowing her to reward herself for responding with a point, counted on a golf counter. However, this approach will be more successful if there is a way of making the social signals more meaningful for the child, rather than expecting the child with autism to understand just through exposure or reward.

Hadwin et al. (1994) and van Berkalear-Onnes (1994) build on the reported capacity to elicit pretend play in this group (e.g. Lewis and Boucher, 1988) by using prompting to train pretend play. Hadwin et al. (1994) were unsuccessful in encouraging play, yet van Berkalear-Onnes (1994) reported some improvements in functional and symbolic play following the training. Interestingly, she started with training simple manipulation and then advanced to the more complex skill of pretend play, which may suggest that some developmental steps are necessary if pretend play is to have any real meaning.

In a recent study by Libby et al. (1996), photographs of children with autism engaged in prompted pretend play were used in an attempt to develop pretence. Developing principles laid out by Powell and Jordan (1993), this study hoped to make the child's sense of agency during pretend play explicit, so that change to spontaneous pretence could be encouraged. Although pretend play was encouraged to an extent, many of the pretend behaviours produced after training were exact replications of acts introduced during the training. Such 'learned' behaviours do have some value in that they make the children with autism more attractive play mates; however, means to encourage spontaneous pretend play remain elusive. It may be that still photographs are not good ways of highlighting the active agency that is necessary for pretend play and a better medium may be the use of mirrors or video. The use of video, and digital camera photographs connected to a computer that can animate them appropriately are currently being used in some schools to help children with autism understand and reflect upon many of their own behaviours, including play. It is too early for evaluation, but teachers report individual examples of limited success in the development of generalised behaviours such as play.

An encouraging use of photographs to encourage play development is happening in some schools and units for children with autism in the UK and elsewhere. Often they feature as part of the work of speech and language therapists and their role is to help the child develop 'story scripts' for pretend play sequences. In this technique, key events in a play drama are photographed and the child is taught to sequence these correctly to unfold the 'story'. This sequence is then used to prompt the actual play sequence and this is practised until the child can perform the play act by following the photographs, otherwise unaided. A more sophisticated variation of this is where more than one child's roles are used in the creation of the story sequence of photographs and so the children learn to wait for one another to take their part at each step in the sequence and to make their actions fit in with those of others. Clearly, this requires a degree of understanding that may only be attainable by the more able children with autism, but simpler versions may enable participation in play events, with all the social benefits that entails, even if it does not lead to full understanding of what is going on.

## Using Play as a Context for Learning

Beyond the development of play itself, play can also be used within the curriculum to develop other skills. Early interactional play can be used to develop social and communicative skills in children with autism. Two examples of such approaches are musical interaction therapy (explored above) and Sherborne (featured in detail in Lord's chapter in this book). Other examples appear in Chapter 9 by Davies on communication.

## Using Role Play and Stories

Some of the social advantages of training pretend play may not be appropriate when considering the needs of older children with autism, but a similar approach can be used in developing abilities to use and comprehend metaphor and humour, both of which relate to the principles first demonstrated in pretend play (McGhee, 1983; Sharrat, 1994). Newson (1992) provides a number of strategies to develop flexibility and social empathy in more able children with autism and Asperger's Syndrome. She describes a number of tasks that explore metaphor, double meaning, imaginative games and make believe worlds. For example, a child may be encouraged to think of a world the other way round. It is clear that these tasks relate to the principles that are first demonstrated in pretend play such as treating objects and situations as if they are something else. Such games may help develop a number of skills including communication, flexibility and imagination.

# Using Group Games

Many teachers will use more formal games to provide leisure skills but also to develop turn-taking, co-operative, competitive and communication skills. Some commercial board games can be chosen, either because they are culturally valid (they are popular with normally developing peers and so provide access to integration and leisure activities) or because they build on a particular interest of the child with autism. Those that are based on logic and/or spatial intelligence (such as chess) may be easier for the child with autism to grasp than those based on social understanding (such as 'Cluedo'). Sometimes popular games can be amended to emphasise particular points that the teacher wants to get across, or whole new games can be developed based on a familiar idea.

An example of this is the game of 'Happy Families', taken from the popular picture card game, which one of the authors developed in her work with children with autism. This amended game was based on objects rather than cards (found to be more motivating and more likely to keep the children 'on task', even for the more able) and was designed to develop classification skills, choice, the use of vocatives to gain attention, appropriate speaker/addressee pronoun use, memory, awareness of other foci of interest and intent and a sense of co-operation. This ambitious list of aims meant that it could be played by a mixed ability group of children with autism (a necessary constraint given the staffing levels and the need to involve a group while other children received one to one teaching), with each of them getting something out of the activity. Where certain steps were beyond the abilities of an individual child, they could be prompted so that the game could continue. Some steps (such as an understanding of classification, hierarchy, and class and exemplar names) were taught individually to the children as 'entry-behaviour' skills for the game.

The game proceeds as follows: The teacher and three to four children sit around a table and each member of the group chooses a class of objects to collect from a pre-determined set presented to the group as a set of pictures. Examples of these sets would be clothes, vehicles, animals, furniture. The set pictures are then removed and each child is given one miniature object representing each of the sets being collected in the game. With the examples given above, then, an individual child might have a doll's dress, a toy lorry, a toy giraffe and a doll's chair placed in a tray in front of him or her while another child might have a doll's shoe, a toy aeroplane, a toy cat and a doll's bed. The first child might have chosen to collect 'animals', while the second might be collecting 'furniture'. Turns progress in order round the table, but each child chooses who to ask for what, from scrutinising the array in front of each child, remembering what they themselves are collecting and also remembering the choice of the other person, in order to offer an appropriate swap.

The final goal format of each child's response is the following, although, as can be imagined, it may take months or years to achieve this fully spontaneously, and this might never be attained by those with severe learning difficulties. Where there is no or little speech, signs or symbols are used, but some means of communication is a necessary pre-skill for participation. Having chosen an addressee (let us assume the first child addressing the second, in our example) the child then says 'X (the child's name), will you swap your cat for my chair?'. Success in this involves, as indicated, knowing who to address (who has still got an animal in front of him or her), using the person's name as a vocative to gain attention before addressing them, using the correct addressee pronouns ('you' and 'your'), recognising and naming the exemplar item (cat) of the class being collected (animals), remembering that that is the class one is collecting, remembering the class the other child is collecting (furniture), recognising and naming the exemplar of that class (chair) and using the correct speaker pronoun ('my'). In addition the child has to recognise when their set is complete (all of the same class) and announce the fact so that he or she can be proclaimed a winner. Rewards are arranged for the group when everyone has a completed set, but it is important that the child develops a sense of competing and the end state to be aimed for.

The game appears more daunting than it actually is, when each step has been carefully taught and structured over a period of time. However, it is not an easy option for a teacher on a rainy afternoon – it involves a demanding teaching role. The teacher has to be aware of the individual goal of the session for each child so that the degree of prompting and guidance can be adjusted accordingly. Performance must be closely monitored and, in addition, the teacher has to engender motivation, providing continual reminders of the final goal to be achieved and the reward that will follow when it has. For some children, the external reward will always be important (and so the game will be less valuable) but experience shows that continual experience of the structured game leading to a predictable end state became motivating in itself, for the majority of children. Anecdotally, there was also some generalisation of the skills learnt in these sessions, although some prompting of the skills in other contexts was usually needed at first.

## Conclusion

Having taken a broad based definition of play we have explored both its place in the autistic condition and suggested some ways of developing play as a context for learning. Clearly, there is much more that could be said and many more examples of the ways in which play is used with children with autism. We do not claim that it will be easy to teach spontaneous play skills to children with autism, nor to develop those they have; if it were easy, it would not be a recognised core problem of autism. What we hope we have shown, is that play can and should be a valuable part of the curriculum for pupils with autism, facilitating all aspects of development – the social, the cognitive, the emotional and the communicative. It also provides a practical context for enabling integration and for teaching basic skills that can be applied in a variety of contexts.

It is hoped that teachers will be supported in playing with pupils with autism and will not feel that this is some 'extra' or trivial activity that can be relegated to extra-curricular time. Rather, we suggest that play is a unique opportunity to bring together all the important facets of the developing personality and to address them as a whole. As such, it deserves a central place in the curriculum. We would also mention that it is fun, but we would not like to give any excuse for ignoring it to those who think that activities (especially in school) can only be valuable if they are tedious!

# References

Atlas, J.A. (1990) 'Play in assessment and intervention in the childhood psychoses', *Child Psychiatry and Human Development*, **21** (2), 119–133.

Balazs, A., Prekop, Cs., Oszi, P., Racz, Zs., Farkas, E. & Stefanik, K. (1996) Beanbag: a specialist framework for social, communication and cognitive training for autistic children, poster presentation at *Therapeutic Intervention in Autism: Perspectives from Research & Practice*, Conference 1-3 April, abstracts published by the Autism Research Unit, University of Sunderland.

Baron-Cohen, S. (1987) 'Autism and symbolic play'. *British Journal of Developmental Psychology*, **5**, 139–148.

Bateson, M.C. (1975) 'Mother-infant exchanges: the epigenesis of conversational interaction', in D. Aaronson, & R.W. Rieber (eds) *Developmental Psycholinguistics and Communication Disorders*. New York: New York Academy of Sciences. pp.101–113.

Belchic, J.K. and Harris, S.L. (1994) 'The use of multiple peer exemplars to enhance the generalisation of play skills to the siblings of children with autism'. *Child and Family Behavior Therapy*, **16** (2), 1–25.

Bornstein, M.H. and O'Reilly, A.W. (eds) (1993) *The Role of Play in the Development of Thought*. San Francisco: Jossey-Bass Publishers.

Bruner, J. (1983) The acquisition of pragmatic commitments In R.M. Golinkoff (ed.) *The Transition form Pre-Linguistic to Linguistic Communication*. Hillslade, NJ: Erlbaum.

Bruner, J. & Feldman, C. (1993) 'Theories of mind and the problem of autism', in S. Baron-Cohen, H. Tager-Flusberg & D.J. Cohen (eds) *Understanding Other*

*Minds: Perspectives from Autism.* Oxford: Oxford University Press.

Christie, P., Newson, E., Newson, J. and Preveser, W. (1992) 'An interactive approach to language and communication for nonspeaking children', in D.A. Lane & A. Miller (eds) *Child and Adolescent Therapy: A Handbook.* Buckingham: Open University Press.

Coe, D.A., Matson, C., Craigie, C.J. and Gossen, M.A. (1991) 'Play skills of autistic children: assessment and instruction'. *Child and Family Behaviour Therapy.* **13** (3), 13–40.

Cooper, J., Moodley, M. & Reynell, J. (1978) *Helping Language Development.* London: Arnold.

Dawson, G. and McKissick, F.C. (1984) Self-recognition in autistic children. *Journal of Autism and Developmental Disorders*, **14**, 383–394.

Dunn, J (1988) *The Beginnings of Social Understanding.* Oxford: Blackwells.

Fein, G.G. (1981) 'Pretend play in childhood: an integrative review'. *Child Development*, **52**, 1095–1118.

Hadwin, J., Baron-Cohen, S., Howlin, P. and Hill, K. (1994) 'Concepts of emotion, belief and pretence: to what extent can these be taught to children with autism'. Unpublished manuscript. London: Institute of Psychiatry.

Happé, F. (1995) 'Do children with autism succumb to visual illusions?. *British Psychological Society Developmental Section Annual Conference*, University of Strathclyde, 8–11 September.

Haring, T.G. and Lovinger, L. (1989) 'Promoting social interaction through teaching generalised play initiation responses to preschool children with autism'. Journal of the Association for Persons with Severe Handicap, **14**, 58–67.

Hobson, R.P. (1993) *Autism and the Development of Mind.* Hove: Lawrence Erlbaum Associates.

Howlin, P. & Rutter, M. (1978) *Treatment of Autistic Children.* Chichester: Wiley.

Jarrold, C., Boucher, J. & Smith, P. (1993) 'Symbolic play in autism: a review', *Journal of Autism and Developmental Disorders*, **23** (2), 281–309.

Jarrold, C., Boucher, J. & Smith, P.K. (1996) Generativity deficits in pretend play in autism'. *British Journal of Developmental Psychology*, **14** (3), 275–300

Jones, G. & Newson, E. (1992) 'Summary of research project funded jointly by the Department of Health and the Department for Education on the provision for children and adults with autism living in England and Wales'. Unpublished report. *Child Development Research Unit*, University of Nottingham, Nottingham.

Jordan, R. (1990) *The Option Approach to Autism: Observer Project Report.* Willesden: National Autistic Society.

Jordan, R.R. (1996) 'Autism and severe learning difficulties', in: R.R. Jordan (ed.) EDSE02 – Special educational needs of pupils with autism Unit 1: The Continuum of Needs and Provision: *Distance Education Course- Autism* (Pupils). University of Birmingham.

Jordan, R.R. & Powell, S.D. (1994) Whose curriculum? Critical notes on integration and entitlement *European Journal of Special Needs Education*, **9**, 27-39.

Jordan, R.R. & Powell, S.D. (in press) 'Therapist drift: identifying a new phenomenon in evaluating therapeutic approaches', in P. Shattock and G.

Lindfoot (eds) *Therapeutic Intervention in Autism: Perspectives from Research and Practice*. University of Sunderland/NAS.

Kaufman, B.N. (1976) *To Love is to be Happy With*. London: Souvenir Press.

Kaufman, B.N. (1994) *Son Rise: the Miracle Continues*. Tiburon, CA: H. J. Kramer Inc.

Koegel, R.L., Firestone, P.B., Kramme, K.W. & Dunlap, G. (1974) 'Increasing spontaneous play by suppressing self-stimulation in autistic children'. *Journal of Applied Behavioural Analysis*, **7**, 521–528.

Leslie, A.M. (1987) 'Pretense and representation: the origins of "theory of mind"', *Psychological Review*, **94** (4), 412–426.

Lewis, V. and Boucher, J. (1988) 'Spontaneous, instructed and elicited play in relatively able autistic children'. *British Journal of Developmental Psychology*, **6**, 325–337.

Libby, S., Powell, S., Messer, D. and Jordan, R. (1995) 'Spontaneous pretend play in children with autism: a reappraisal'. *British Psychological Society Developmental Section Annual Conference*, University of Strathclyde, 8–11 April.

Libby, S., Messer, D., Jordan, R. and Powell, S. (1996) 'Using photographs to encourage spontaneous pretend play in children with autism'. *5th International Congress Autism-Europe*, Barcelona, 3–5 May.

McGhee, P. (1983) 'Humor development: towards a life span approach', in P.McGhee and J.Goldstein (eds) *Handbook of Humor Research: Vol.1. Basic Issues*. New York: Springer-Verlag.

Meltzoff, A. & Gopnik, A. (1993) 'The role of imitation in understanding persons and developing a theory of mind', in S. Baron-Cohen, H. Tager-Flusberg & D.J. Cohen (eds) *Understanding Other Minds: Perspectives from Autism*. Oxford: Oxford University Press.

Newson, J. (1979) 'The growth of shared understandings between infant and caregiver', in M. Bullowa (ed.) *Before Speech*. Cambridge: Cambridge University Press.

Newson, E. (1992) 'Enabling flexibility and social empathy in able autistic children: some practical strategies'. Unpublished manuscript. University of Nottingham.

Newson, E. (1996) *Effective Learning and Teaching: Current Interventions in Autism: Some Contrasting Perspectives*. Distance Education: Autism Pupils Course Text. University of Birmingham.

Nind, M. & Hewett, D. (1994) *Access to Communication*. London: David Fulton.

Park, C.C. (1986) 'Social growth in autism: a parent's perspective', in E. Schopler & G.B. Mesibov (eds) *Social Behaviour in Autism*. New York: Plenum Press.

Perner, J. (1991) *Understanding the Representational Mind*. London: MIT Press.

Powell, S.D. and Jordan, R.R. (1993) 'Being subjective about autistic thinking and learning to learn'. *Educational Psychology*, **12** (3 & 4), 359–370.

Prevezer, W. (1990) 'Strategies for tuning in to autism'. *Therapy Weekly*, 18 October, 4.

Riguet, C.B., Taylor, N.D., Benaroya, S. and Klein, L.S. (1981) 'Symbolic play in autistic, Down's and normal children of equivalent mental age'. *Journal of Autism and Developmental Disorders*, **11**, 439–448.

Roeyers, H. (1995) 'Peer-mediated interventions to facilitate the social interactions of children with a pervasive developmental disorder'. *British Journal of Special Education*, 22, 161–164.

Roeyers, H. and van Berkalaer-Onnes, I.A. (1994) 'Play in autistic children'. *Communication and Cognition*, **27** (3), 349–359.

Russell, J. (1994) 'Agency and early mental development'. In J. Bermudez, A. J. Marcel & N. Eilan (eds) *The Body and the Self.* Cambridge, MA: MIT Press.

Sharratt, P.A. (1994) 'A postulated theoretical relationship between the metaphor production and pretend play of young children'. *British Psychological Society Annual Conference*, Brighton, 24–27. March

Shotter, J. and Newson, J. (1974) 'How babies communicate'. *New Society*, **29**, 346–347.

Sigman, M. and Ungerer, J.A. (1984) 'Cognitive and language skills in autistic, mentally retarded, and normal children'. *Developmental psychology*, **20**, 293–302.

Stahmer, A.C. (1995) 'Teaching symbolic play skills to children with autism using pivotal response training'. *Journal of Autism and Developmental Disorders*, **25** (2), 123–141.

Stahmer, A.C. and Schreibman, L. (1992) 'Teaching children with autism appropriate play in an unsupervised environment using a self-management treatment package'. *Journal of Applied Behaviour Analysis*, **25** (2), 447–459.

Thorp, D.M., Stahmer, A.C. and Screibman, L. (1995) 'Effects of sociodramatic play training on children with autism'. *Journal of Autism and Developmental Disorders*, **25** (3), 265–282.

Tiegerman, E. and Primavera, L. (1981) 'Object manipulation: an interactional strategy'. *Journal of Autism and Developmental Disorders*, **11** (4), 427–438.

Tilton, J.R. and Ottinger, D.R. (1964) 'Comparison of the toy play behavior of autistic, retarded and normal children'. *Psychological Reports*, **15**, 967–975.

Ungerer, J.A. and Sigman, M. (1981) 'Symbolic play and language comprehension in autistic children'. *Journal of the Academy of Child Psychiatry*, **20**, 318–337.

van Berkalaer-Onnes, I.A. (1994) 'Play training for autistic children', in J.Hellendorn, R.van der Kooij and B.Sutton-Smith (eds) *Play and Intervention*. New York: State University of New York Press.

Watson, L.R. (1985) 'The TEACCH communication curriculum', in E. Schopler & G.B. Mesibov (eds) *Communication Problems in Autism*. New York: Plenum Press.

Whyte, J. and Owens, A. (1989) 'Language and symbolic play: some findings from a study of autistic children'. *Journal of Speech and Hearing Research*, **27**, 364–377.

Williams, D. (1996) *Autism: An Inside Out Approach*. London: Jessica Kingsley.

Wimpory, D., Chadwick, P. & Nash, S. (1995) 'Musical interaction therapy for children with autism: an evaluation case study with a two-year follow up. *Journal of Autism and Developmental Disorders*, **25**, 541–552

Wing, L., Gould, J., Yeates, S. & Brierly, L. (1977) 'Symbolic play in severely mentally retarded and in autistic children'. *Journal of Child Psychology and*

*Psychiatry*, **18**, 167–178.

Wooten, M. & Mesibov, G.B. (1986) 'Social skills training for elementary school autistic children with normal peers', in E. Schopler & G.B. Mesibov (eds) *Social Behaviour in Autism*. New York: Plenum Press.

Wulff, S.B. (1985) 'The symbolic and object play of children with autism: a review'. *Journal of Autism and Developmental Disorders*, **15**, 139–148.

# CHAPTER 4

# Beyond compliance: The importance of group work in the education of children and young people with autism

Margaret M. Golding

## Introduction

There is a growing need for appropriate facilities for children with autism. At present in the UK there are approximately three autistic children for every specialist place available and this has led to greater efforts by the authorities to include more children in schools other than those catering specifically for their needs. The philosophy of inclusion has much to commend it, but if it is to work for the benefit of children with autism, it is essential that the nature of the disability is understood and that the curriculum on offer is able to be accessed by them.

From the early literature on autism, it seemed to the handful of teachers working in the field that the most important goal was to establish a relationship with the child and sadly, it was often thought that if one waited long enough, the child would eventually emerge from his/her autistic state. The assumption then was that learning would take place in the usual way. This meant that much time and effort was put into 1:1 teaching and learning, and this required a very high staffing ratio. It was soon realised that this was not the whole story and that the children did not seem to learn in the same way as other children. Teachers observed that waiting for such a child to be ready and motivated to learn might mean waiting forever. They noted that the children had sensorial and perceptual difficulties (Hermelin and O'Connor, 1964 a, and b) which got in the way of learning and that they required a different style of teaching to take account of their difficulties (Clark, 1965).

In the last three decades there has been an explosion of research and theorising which has concentrated on how children with autism think and learn (Baron-Cohen et al.,1985; Jordan and Powell, 1995) and some able adults with autism have written accounts of what it was like for them as children (Grandin and Scarrano, 1986; Williams, 1996). What comes over so strongly from their writings is the need to respect the differences and the strengths of the person with autism. Williams, in particular, writes about the harm that the stereotyping of people with autism has done and suggests that professionals and parents remain the spokespeople for those with autism and that people with autism, like herself, are seen as exceptions.

It was this sort of thinking which led me to consider some years ago how best we could assist some of our older students to move beyond compliance. We wished to find effective ways to develop the confidence and self advocacy skills which would reduce their vulnerability and enable them to continue to grow and learn after they left their specialist school. The school had a reputation for giving the children and young people a high quality educational experience and we felt that they were leaving us with a good range of skills. Perhaps we were most proud of the fact that although the majority of our children had come to the residential school because of their extreme challenging behaviours and were often a danger to themselves and others, they left us as compliant and calm students. We prided ourselves on the fact that on outings to the theatre or other community events with a group of teenagers, we would often be told by members of the public how beautifully behaved the young people were.

This in itself, should perhaps have been a warning as normally teenage groups are not noted for their calm and passive behaviour! At that time, on leaving school, most of the students were able to proceed to an adult community for people with autism. It was only when reports started filtering through from these placements that we began to question our educational approaches and to ask ourselves what it was that we were not doing. The communities reported that our students were very easy to manage but they had not many skills. This was not the picture we had seen at the school. Put quite simply, what had happened was that the students were waiting to be told what to do in their new surroundings. They were far too compliant. We realised that the 'well behaved' young person with autism was characterised by excessive dependency on parents and keyworkers and was in fact, behaving exactly in the way that Williams has so recently described.

In discussions with colleagues, we began to reflect on just why it was that our young people had been unable to generalise their skills into their new environments. We immediately realised that their excessive dependency meant that without adult cues, the students did not have the confidence to initiate or even carry out familiar tasks and thus appeared as passive or lazy. We explored the concepts of confidence, self advocacy and self esteem and made a decision to actively try and develop these aspects of the student's personality. We then had to create the environment in which these goals could be achieved.

## Creating a Peer Group

In normal development the peer group provides an important stepping stone to individual autonomy. In observing our students we became aware that the young person with autism needs help to create a peer group. This is not something to be left until the teenage years. We know now that it must start the moment a child comes to school. Each day as they come into school the youngest children are persuaded to sit in a group and pick up a book until everyone arrives. The circle of chairs is such that children are placed as near to another child as they can tolerate. If they wander away, they are gently brought back. The focus is on the book and not on the seating arrangements and, with daily repetition, the children begin to tolerate the close physical proximity and become less oversensitive to physical contact. From this, the children then move onto a whole group activity such as responding to their photographs and names or a singing game.

We are aware from the accounts of many of our older students that they had great problems with touching and physical contact in general. While longing on the one hand to be held or touched, on the other hand they had a terrible fear of it. Temple Grandin in the animated film 'A for Autism' talks of her need for physical contact but her fear of being swallowed up by it. We know that she had to create a sense of being held for herself and built a squeeze machine to fulfil this function (Grandin, 1992).

Movement lessons within the physical education curriculum which are based on the work of Veronica Sherborne and involve trust and weight bearing exercises, lead to body awareness. They also help to encourage physical interaction and the understanding of physical boundaries within experiences which are non-threatening and pleasurable (Sherborne, 1990). Throughout the day, children are worked in pairs. They go for walks with their partners and take messages in twos. Watching the young people engaged in this activity is to appreciate their very real difficulties. So many factors are involved in walking with someone next to them, not in front or behind and with just the right space. Pupils are encouraged to monitor each other and let the partner know how to get it right.

In giving simple instructions to the children, teachers will try to promote communication by moving away from the star shaped interaction of the authoritarian group centred on the keyworker and will 'jet drive' the interactions through a peer, e.g. 'John, ask Mary to close the door'. This means the children have to look at each other and listen as well. They also have to persevere, but as children with autism seem to enjoy giving instructions to one another as much as other young children, this technique is often successful in establishing a limited form of group interaction.

One of the challenges in trying to create a peer group is how to get recognition from it for an individual who is profoundly handicapped. Giving power to this student over the rest of the group is, in itself, a powerful tool. It seems that one of the most important tasks which is guaranteed to get everyone's attention is serving food. If the teacher appears to be doing something else, the students have to give the server some pretty strong signals if he is to get the portions right! They also have to give him some respect and thanks and the positive effects are visible immediately. Where the student is part of a discussion and lacks communication skills, it is useful to ask other members of the group how they think the student is feeling or what choices they think he might like to make. Regular practice in this type of activity soon demonstrates that the students with autism can show empathy and that they make great efforts to try and understand their more handicapped peers with remarkable results. One student whose speech is totally unintelligible to adults, is understood by his peers who are often in the role of interpreters.

Choices give the individual status and power over the group. On an outing he can be asked, 'this way or that way?'. If democratic decision making is instituted then it is one person's turn to decide, and the rest must follow. Opportunities for choice should be sought for and thought about when the teacher is planning programmes. From the earliest years, restricted choices can be offered and this can be built upon so that the young person is given a feeling of autonomy and is helped to develop his self-advocacy skills. With choice comes responsibility and the child quickly learns that once a choice is made, he is stuck with it. This ensures that the child begins to get an idea of consequences, a concept which is known to be difficult for children with autism.

## Preparing for Group Events

### The birthday party

The birthday party package is a part of the curriculum not usually found in school. However, for young children with autism this programme is a valuable tool in the formation of a peer group. Many children with autism are invited to a birthday party once only and if this is not remedied they do feel isolated and different at a later age when their siblings are invited to parties and they are left out. The teacher will teach and practice the skills needed for a birthday party. This usually includes eating off a paper plate (your own), drinking from a paper cup and playing a party game such as 'pass the parcel'. Parents are very much involved in the programme and when the skills are learned the first party takes place at school with the family invited. As the children experience a number of birthday parties and the skills improve, the next step is for the party to happen at home. This initially takes place at lunchtime and the whole class attends. Once this is established and everyone feels confident, the family will run the party itself and invite the other members of the class and their parents. As the years go by, not only do the pupils have a peer group, but so do the parents who come to know and share each other's children.

## Interpersonal Activities

With young children there are plenty of pleasurable activities and games which are legitimate and which lend themselves to interactive approaches. Finger games and singing games with a surprise touch at the end can be used as well as tickling and chasing games. Here, the teacher may set up the game so that the children also play the teacher's role thus taking a proactive part in the activity. With older students, there is a need to find a legitimate way to set up these experiences. We found it useful to talk about 'messing about', and even put this on their schedules, thus creating opportunities for interactive physical play. We observed the sort of horseplay that goes on with adolescents and set up a situation for instance, when everyone was sitting on a bench and the teacher who was sitting on the end, engineered it that by a little pushing the person on the end fell off. The initial reaction by the group was one of seriousness and shock but when this happened once or twice it began to be seen as a 'bit of fun' and was tolerated accordingly. Such activities require much reflection and sensitivity on the part of the teacher, who has to bear in mind the personalities of the pupils in his/her group.

Every activity offers opportunities for group interaction of a meaningful kind and it is what goes on between the people involved which determines the quality. In other words, what the teacher says and the way in which it is said, determines the nature of the relationship. This in turn, determines the basic mode of intervention. Every shared experience, however small, can be the vehicle of communication. Thus the teacher will either help or hinder, care or not care, but perhaps most importantly, the teacher can demonstrate authority over the student or set the scene for self responsibility and self development.

## Peer Tutoring and Induction

We have seen how the person with autism as described by Williams (1996), often presents either as locked into a set of reactive mannerisms or as a dreadful parody of the adult demands that have been made on him or her. Neither of these modes of behaviour as we have learned, bodes well for successful placement in later life. The 'compartmentalised' learning of children with autism often means that they learn a skill in one situation, which they seem unable to transfer to another. If this is not understood it can lead to tensions between staff and parents and the community to which a young person may transfer.

One way of helping the young person to overcome this, is to adopt an implicit model of teaching in which the learner occupies first a reactive, and then a dominant role as if the performance comes partly from a kind of internalised dialogue. This model can usefully be adapted to other tasks where the child is in the dominant role and the teacher later withdraws and is replaced by a peer. In taking the learning a step forward in this way, by the nature of the task, the child seems to analyse its essential components and absorb them, enabling him then to transfer the skills to another situation. For instance, when teaching young children to cross the road, the teacher will analyse the task and teach the skills in the usual way. The next step will be for the child to teach the teacher how to cross the road and the final step will be for the teacher to withdraw and the child to teach another pupil. Once this process has been worked through, the child will be able to cross most roads in different situations. Using these approaches with a group, results in the children taking an interest in each other's performance and often identifying with it as though they are undertaking a mental rehearsal.

When the young people arrive at their final years in school and join a 'Leavers' Group' there are valuable opportunities to put them in charge of their learning. Rather than having a period of induction organised and run by the staff, it has been found that a peer tutoring model of induction enables the older students to assess their own level of skill and to take responsibility for the success (or otherwise) of another student. Thus, second year students are paired with new first year students. The senior student is responsible for welcoming the new student, showing him around and making sure he feels OK. Initially, the new student will shadow him as he refers to the jobs list on the wall and carries out his duties. Gradually, the new student will learn to carry them out correctly. It is essential that the senior student gives him empathy and support or he is set up for failure.

These concepts are explored and discussed in the weekly counselling groups which take place during the two years of the Leavers programme and they are uppermost in the older students' minds. Nevertheless, they often still need to be helped to reflect on the new students feelings from time to time. This is done by the senior student asking the younger student how he feels, by giving him regular praise, by paying compliments and by informal discussion with members of staff who are their mentors during this period.

During these periods of induction, staff have observed how older students have been affected by role models. Many of the students when teaching their junior peers initially adopt staff mannerisms and approaches, sometimes with uncanny accuracy. However, the mimicry gradually fades and as they apparently become more skilled in their teaching role the students find their own styles. Working in this way at the beginning of the Leavers year means that there is already a strong bond between students at the end of their induction and staff have observed how the senior students spontaneously support the other students thereafter.

There are many ways to extend the students experience by peer tutoring. It has been found valuable in a school which uses the Makaton system of augmentative communication to give a group of students the opportunity each year to undertake an intensive Peer Tutors course. The students are usually very good at the signing and symbols but struggle with the concept of teaching someone who is disabled in other ways or who is angry and frightened. However, they do manage to cope with these roles and when they have the qualification, the school is able to provide them with work experience with younger children both in the day and residential settings.

## Developing Empathy for Others

The work of the Leavers group focuses very strongly on the development of empathy. There is continual reference to feelings, with students identifying their own feelings as well as those of the others. The group is encouraged to use peer group pressure to modify unacceptable behaviours. It may be that an activity is stopped or the group will come together in unstructured time to consider the actions of one of its members. The group soon becomes articulate about its views of the other person's behaviour and the disapproval of the group has a powerful influence on the student concerned. The students seems to find great joy in group activities and group support and do not like to be excluded from it at this stage.

In the same way, achievement is celebrated by the group and again, this is a very powerful motivator and reinforcer. On many occasions, the group has praised the performance of one of its members who had undertaken a chore with great reluctance. One student who complained about having to learn and undertake the task of washing up was applauded by the whole group in a counselling meeting after he had completed the task. He was delighted by this and subsequently informed the group that he had now undertaken all the washing up at home, for which of course, he received more applause! Applause is a powerful reinforcer and can be used effectively by the group to draw their attention to the smallest achievements by its members.

Even though empathy seems to be established when students are engaged with each other, it is not always evident in their dealings with other people and more work has to be done to help students become aware that staff have feelings too! Often the students seem very egocentric, but when exploring this it has become evident that the students think that the adults around them know everything, even sometimes what they are thinking. They are always very surprised in the counselling group when discussing what they are good at and what they need help with, and they hear staff members talk about their difficulties. There is inevitably amazement and then following that, amusement, and continuing references to the fact that there is something a member of staff cannot do. This is particularly evident when it happens to be a skill which most students with autism have a flair for, e.g. map reading!

## Autonomous Group Functioning

One of the problems faced by groups of young people with autism is getting other people to relate to them as a group. This is especially so on educational outings where there may be the services of a guide or a curator. It is often necessary for the staff to stand back a little and avoid giving the guide much eye contact so that he will eventually interact with the young people instead of looking for cues from the teacher. The staff need to brief the students to walk with the guide and to look after their partners. Success is when the guide and group are far ahead and it is the staff lagging behind!

In order to know whether a peer group has truly been created it is necessary to withdraw the adult and observe how the group functions on its own. It is easy to make assumptions about the young people's skills but these assumptions are almost always based on performance when the adult is present. For instance, in rehearsing three girls who were making a Spanish omelette, the assistants observed a competent performance within a reasonable time span. The next day the girls repeated the activity this time without their own staff but with a student who was known to them, videoing. She had been asked not to cue the students but found the task very difficult, although the students did not ask for help and were able to demonstrate all the correct skills, they looked to her for a cue at each part of the process. The result was that the making of the omelette took the best part of three hours. In viewing the video, the girls knew exactly what they had not done quickly enough and where they had lost their confidence. It was a painful experience for them and the staff, and yet when they repeated the activity after watching and discussing the video they had a very good result. The use of video for improving performance is a very effective tool, but needs to be used sensitively with lots of humour and support if the students are to remain confident.

Independent working within the group can be started at an early age. The TEACCH programme has proved to be a valuable approach in this regard (Schopler, 1989). Children are taught to use a visual schedule thus using their preferred mode of learning. They gain experience of independent working by first working alone with simple tasks they can already do, at a distraction free work station. Gradually, they are able to work independently from the teacher and alongside another child. Eventually, they are able to work independently within the group. This process builds up the child's confidence and a work ethic is established which will stand him in good stead in later life. This method can also be used to assist the student with autism to improve the volume and pace of his work, an aspect of performance which is difficult even for the more able students.

## Dealing with Emotions

By the time the students are ready to leave school and make a transition to a college or community, we need to be sure that not only have we put them in charge of their behaviour and learning, but that we have helped them to be in charge of their feelings. We know from their own accounts how difficult it is for children with autism to make sense of emotion. We know that many of the children are in states of high arousal akin to severe anxiety (Hutt and Hutt, 1970). Bettelheim in his book, *The Informed Heart* (1960) dealing with the effects of the concentration camp, writes of the horrific examples of the destructive and disintegrative forces of anxiety on the human personality. He likened children with autism to the concentration camp victims in this regard. Even when talking about anxiety in normal young children, Bettelheim conveys just how devastating an effect it can have. He describes how, if the child is acutely anxious then he is no longer sure what he really did. He tells us that it often forces children to believe they did something right when they did wrong as it sometimes forces them to believe they have done wrong when they haven't.

Bettelheim we now know was wrong in his views on the causation of autism, and there is doubt about the value of his treatment approach. Nevertheless, the picture he paints is not unfamiliar to those who work with autism. The challenge is to find strategies which are effective in lowering the high arousal level. We need to help the young people to increase their emotional range and help with the recognition and legitimisation of their feelings, as well as develop their sense of being valued members of the group. This, in our experience, has resulted in a more positive self image and improved performance and transfer of learning.

# Group Counselling

One such way is to use group counselling to assist the students with autism to reflect on their situation and to share their feelings and experiences with others. It has been useful to create a structure for these counselling sessions with which the students become familiar and comfortable. Simple but effective principles should be adhered to so that the activity has status and is seen to be protected from minor changes to the timetable. If there has to be a change either on the part of the counsellor or because the students wish it then that is brought to the group so that everyone is aware of the situation. Thus, the group takes place at the same time each week for about 75 minutes. Staff are invited to become equal members of the group and to contribute in the same way as the students.

At the beginning of the year when the group has some new members, the students take part in an exercise to increase their awareness of the 'listening posture'. Thereafter the young person who is speaking will scan the group to check that body language is appropriate and that everyone is focused on him. The group always starts with a positive statement from each member in answer to the question 'What was good for you this week?'. The end of the session is likewise positive and usually finishes with either an idea to look forward to, or positive reinforcement from the counsellor. There is room in the session for personal difficulties to be articulated and the emphasis is on sharing and identifying feelings rather than on magical solutions. The counselling group very soon becomes 'special' to the young people who often make reference to it during the week and invariably check to make sure it is happening even though they know it is sacrosanct.

Once the sharing of good things at the beginning of the session has happened, there is work to be done and this requires the students to work together and speak for each other. It has been found useful to provide visual structure and so the counsellor may hand everyone a printed or symbolised question. In the beginning this will be something simple such as 'What is your favourite food?'. The students will not, however, answer for themselves but working in twos or small groups, they will endeavour to find out from their peers what their favourite food is. Once these little buzz groups have finished then each person in turn, will feed back information gained from peers. This is not as easy as it sounds. Because of their short-term memory difficulties and their egocentricity, it often happens that by the time the student's turn has come around, he or she feeds back what his or her favourite food is rather than that of peers. Very often the student cannot remember what has been said, and the group breaks for a little more buzz group work so that the student can remind him/herself and hold on to the information.

Over the period of the two years that they are in the Leavers' Group, the students improve dramatically in their ability to remember and feed back quite complex information. This technique is used to explore many of the areas which the young people need to know about. To assist them with their self-advocacy skills, 'disability' and 'autism' are tackled. Students are given all the vocabulary that the staff feel might be used about them in the future. They have all had the experience of being talked about in their presence and often can recall words which are used about them such as 'learning difficulties', 'communication difficulties' and 'challenging behaviours'. They are pleased to understand what is meant and even more delighted to learn that everyone has some sort of learning difficulty!

One of the aspects of learning which has become clear from the counselling sessions, is that the young people have become adept at learning pieces of appropriate social behaviour or 'scripts' which enable them to appear socially competent. However, what they do not know are the rules which underpin these areas of functioning. They then find it difficult to know if they are behaving appropriately in situations other than the ones they are used to. This includes such activities as holding doors for people, choosing where and how to sit in a car and interacting with strangers. A recent questionnaire elicited 'Yes' in answer to most questions about how to behave, but 'No' to 'Do you know the rules about this?'. It will be interesting to see if analysing the rules may assist some of the students to generalise their skills more confidently. Group affect is an area that we have recently begun to explore, i.e. how to get an appropriate affective response from the group. Humour is an invaluable tool and using it in the group situation helps students to develop responses which are usual in everyday life. There is a need for the students to experience gentle teasing and to understand that teasing and jokes are part of the adult life they are moving to. Starting with ponderous riddles and jokes the group can enjoy the development of a shared vocabulary of humorous topics and responses.

Counselling takes on board all the rites of passage and the difficulty in leaving a school where the student may have spent his whole school life, is aired from the start and explored throughout the two years. The aim is that having externalised and shared their anxieties about leaving the students will be able to be joyful and excited about the next placement and take their baggage with them.

## Conclusion

All this, and much more, describes the affective nature of the curricular task and the use of group work in a school for young people with autism. The task is to take the students as far as possible along the road to autonomy, so that in his future life they can harness the resources of the group, reduce the risks of things being done *to* them or *for* them all the time, but thus ensure that they are done *by* them.

## Acknowledgements

I should like to acknowledge the contributions of my colleague, Peter Whitehouse, who supported the development of my first Leavers' unit and the staff of Heathlands and Linden Bridge Schools whose commitment and expectations have expanded and enriched the curriculum for pupils with autism.

## References

Baron-Cohen S., Leslie A.M. and Frith, U. (1985) 'Does the autistic child have a theory of mind?'. *Cognition,* **21**, 37–46.

Bettelheim, L. (1960) *The Informed Heart.* Harmondworth: Free Press.

Clark, G.D. (1965) 'An educational programme for psychotic children', in P.T. Weston (ed.) *Some Approaches to Teaching Autistic Children.* London: Pergamon Press.

Grandin, T. (1992) 'An insider's view of autism', in E. Schopler and G. Mesibov (eds) *High Functioning Individuals with Autism.* New York: Plenum Press.

Grandin, T. and Scarrano, M. (1986) *Emergence Labelled Autistic.* London: Costello.

Hermelin, B. and O'Connor, N. (1964a) 'Crossmodal transfer in normal, sub-normal and autistic children'. *Neuropsychologia ,* **2**, 229.

Hermelin, B. and O'Connor, N. (1964b) Effects of sensory input and sensory dominance on severely disturbed autistic children and on subnormal controls'. *British Journal of Psychology*, **55**, 2.

Hutt, S.J. & Hutt, C. (1970) *Behaviour Studies in Psychiatry.* Oxford: Pergamon Press.

Jordan, R.R. and Powell, S.D. (1995) *Understanding and Teaching Children with Autism.* Chichester: Wiley.

Kanner, L. (1943) 'Autistic disturbances of affective contact'. *Nervous Children* **2**, 217–280.

Schopler, E. (1989) 'Principles for directing both education treatment and research', in C. Gilberg (ed.) *Diagnosis & Treatment of Autism.* New York: Plenum Press.

Sherborne, V. (1990) *Development Movement for Children.* Cambridge: Cambridge University Press.

Williams, D. (1996) *Autism: An Inside Out Approach.* London: Jessica Kingsley.

## COMMENTARY

## Containment or Education?

In this chapter Golding draws attention to the dangers that educationists face if they come to believe too readily in their own success. She recalls how in her schooling of children with autism the initial need to *control* so that education could take place needed to be considered in its true light: as a means to other ends rather than as an end in itself. Certainly, we can use methodologies that will make our pupils more compliant. But compliance can create as many difficulties for effective living in the world as can resistance. And for those with autism, for whom social negotiation is fundamentally difficult, compliance can be become an attractive, self-perpetuating response within social scenario.

On occasions when individuals with autism seem to be trying to please their teacher then the reasons may not be those of wanting praise or other social motivations but rather may simply derive from a desire to be left alone. If the demands of the task are too great for the individual to understand then reactions will range from retreat into self-interests or violent rejection of the source of the demand. On the other hand, when the task can be understood then doing it and getting it out of the way is most likely to reduce the pressure of demand from the teacher (demand here may refer 'merely' to social presence). In short, teachers need to recognise the source of the compliance and avoid an over-hasty description of it in terms of an outcome of successful teaching.

## Using Group Dynamics

Golding shows how to use the dynamics that operate within groups in a way that at face value seems surprising. In autism there is a difficulty in understanding how others may be thinking and feeling so it can be assumed that there will be a subsequent difficulty in understanding what the 'feeling of the group' is. Yet in her discussion of the way in which the Leavers' group develops empathy Golding shows how students can come to understand the feeling of the group, they can be responsive to others' reactions. We should be wary of the ever present danger of underestimating the abilities of those with autism or perhaps of misinterpreting them. Children with autism *do* react to the social messages of others, but they may have to work out those messages; they have difficulty at the level of direct perceptual awareness of social signals. What Golding's description tells us is that what is necessary in terms of teaching is that we make our, and their, 'inner' mental states explicit.

## Analysis of Group Functioning

Golding shows how you need to unravel the functions that groups normally fulfil and then devise situations in which children with autism can develop the skills that will enable them to derive the functional benefits. The art is in the way in which the autistic way of thinking is interpreted and then (i) compensated for and (ii) employed to advantage. For example, on the one hand problems of over-sensitivity are dealt with by measured steps of familiarity and on the other the apparent enjoyment of giving instructions is used as a way into learning about communication.

## Making Choices

Golding shows that, although choice presents difficulty for children with autism, it is important not only because it gives status and power within group situations but also because it is an essential for further learning. The overall goal of education should be to produce independent thinkers capable of operating as effectively as possible in society. What Golding suggests in a number of her examples is a structure which makes overt (and, therefore, apparent to the individual) the reflection that is involved in making choices. Autistic learning is necessarily of an artificial kind, but Golding shows how such artificiality can become acceptable within an imaginative learning environment which is responsive to learning needs in autism.

In a similar way, when Golding describes ways of helping the individual with autism to overcome the compartmentalisation of knowledge she is talking about externalising a process of 'dialogue' which in non-autistic thinking is internal. She sets out a way of structuring the interaction so as to enable the child to do out loud and with deliberateness what the non-autistic child would do 'naturally'. Again, the reader may wonder if this does not result in a kind of learning that is perhaps stilted and artificial. The dilemma for the teacher is that there may be a sense in which this is necessarily so in autism. The learning environment can be designed to be in part remedial (in terms of making the autistic learner's thinking more effective) but it also needs to be accommodating (in terms of meeting needs inherent in the way autistic individuals think about the world). Golding's suggested procedure of making the child teach the teacher is a further step in this same process. It enables the child to set up an overt model which describes an operation, in the particular case in this chapter, that of crossing the road.

## When Not to Intervene

Golding gives a very good example of the need for the teacher to 'withdraw' at certain points in any learning situation and the attendant difficulty in autism. There is a sense in which the individual with autism can, unintentionally, draw the teacher into ever more 'supportive' behaviour which feeds the dependency of the learner. Learning when not to intervene is a most significant aspect of learning how to teach and care for children with autism. Even at basic levels such as eye contact, for example, making the child dependent on you as a teacher may create more instances where eye contact is made by the child, but Golding shows how such a phenomenon is delusory; often in autism real learning takes place when the teacher does not intervene. The corollary to this of course is that the teacher has to have set up appropriate structures at the outset if this 'hands off' approach is to work.

## Being 'in Charge of Own Feelings'

There are real difficulties in trying to deal with individuals with autism in a counselling mode. The individual needs first to learn to recognise their own emotional states before they can be engaged in a discovery of (self) meaning and control. Again, Golding shows a way through this difficulty by using the power of the group learning situation. In recognising the aspects of thinking style that will present difficulties (e.g. 'short term memory difficulties and egocentricity') she is able to construct a situation in terms of timing as well as structure that accommodates to that style while pressing for new understandings in terms of self and relationship with others. What her example shows, among other things, is that the notion of counselling in autism needs to emphasise what should be a key feature of any counselling situation. That is, that counsellors need to monitor and strive to understand their own feelings if they are to help clients to do the same with theirs.

In autism, the onus is very much on the teacher/counsellor to examine closely how and why they are responding in a learning situation. Because autism provokes a deviant pattern of social interaction, it requires that the teacher/counsellor be very aware of what they need to do in themselves in order to enable learning in the pupil/client. This is a reversal of the typical teacher approach which requires emphasis on an interpretation of how the learner is behaving and responding. In short, what Golding illustrates here is the need for teachers in autism to be self-reflective in the first instance. They need to ask the question 'why am I behaving in the way I am'? before they can begin to answer the question 'how can I enable a particular pattern of learning to occur in this pupil ?'.

# CHAPTER 5

# The teaching of science

Pam Maddock

## Introduction

In most schools within the primary age range science has been a developing part of the curriculum during recent years. All schools, including special schools, have had to think very carefully about providing appropriate facilities, staff who are able to teach science, and resources specific to the subject. Not only has there been much competition for timetabling but also considerable discussion regarding philosophy and pedagogy, and a great deal has been achieved.

Science has always been about understanding the world around us. For children *without* autism discovering things for themselves, experimenting and 'doing' has for some years been accepted as one of the ways of acquiring a knowledge and understanding of the world. Hence, the predilection for experiential learning in recent educational philosophy. However, as we now know, children with autism have great difficulty with most of the processes which are involved in science: hypothesising, predicting, experimenting, communicating, explaining, classifying and planning. Even if children with autism have no apparent difficulty in 'doing', or completing an activity, teachers have to question how meaningful individual activities are for the child.

This chapter aims to highlight some of the ways in which children with autism can access the science curriculum. Methods are used which not only enable the child to participate but also help children to be in charge of their own learning in a similar way to their non-autistic peers. It is up to us as educators not only to find appropriate ways of presenting science to children with autism but also to make it an enjoyable and useful process. The way science is taught presents itself as a unique opportunity to link the environment and our surroundings to every other part of the curriculum. It can be a medium which promotes communication, allows problem solving, helps pupils with maths and motivates them to engage in art and technology. It should not be seen as a subject in isolation but one which interrelates with every other subject within the curriculum.

## Aims and Purposes of Teaching Science

Any school undertaking the responsibility of teaching science to pupils, of whatever age, should aim to do so in ways which are appropriate to those pupils' needs and abilities. Many of the typical aims of a science curriculum (for example: to help pupils solve problems, to enable them to communicate their results, to give experience of life and living processes and to help pupils record their observations and measurements in various and increasingly complex ways) will present difficulties for people with autism. However, with skilful organisation, careful planning and a knowledge of the individual child much of the science curriculum can be accessed.

## Looking at Psychology and Science

In order to determine specific ways of teaching it may be useful to look at the work of certain writers in psychology so that we are able to structure the environment appropriately for people with autism to work scientifically.

### Man as 'scientist'

If we consider how most people spend their lives it is by experimenting, usually unintentionally and sub-consciously. When we embark on new situations and experiences we try to imagine how the reality will be and endeavour to predict how it will affect our lives. How frightening life must be for people with autism if they are unable to do this. When we start a new job or go to a party we sometimes try to imagine who will be there or what might happen. If we look at life in a similar way to Kelly (1955) we could hypothesise that we as human beings view the world in the way that scientists do. We have a theory about something (a new job) and we see if things happen in the way we predict they would (the experiment or testing the theory). We evaluate the situation and learn from it, then we formulate a new theory. Claxton (1984) suggests that the process of testing and improving our personal theories that guide us through life is what we call learning. We hypothesise, we experiment, test the theory, discard it or accept it and thus go on to develop further personal theories.

If people with autism inherently have difficulty with these processes, then any new situation or learning 'event' is going to be ultimately confusing and new learning may not take place. This chapter aims to look at practical ways which the child with autism can use to function in life as 'scientifically' as possible. It is important that we are aware when teaching any subject, especially science, that the things we remember most about an event are the things that are most meaningful to us. For example, a girl with autism may go on a day visit to the zoo. When asked to relate what she liked most, she may say that she liked the fan in the ladies toilet the best. The challenge therefore, when teaching science is to intuitively seek out ways of enabling children to develop a way of memorising that is more useful and meaningful for future learning. This is important in science as it helps us relate one experiment with another. It is also essential for generalising and applying experiences. Memory for us all is extremely selective. We tune in to events or parts of an event and ultimately in doing this de-select other incidents to do with the occasion. Children with autism need to be helped to reconstruct relevant facts relating to any situation.

It is difficult for a pupil with autism to maintain and adapt to differing situations when the world and the people in it are constantly changing. Teachers are often heard to say, 'Well, he could do that [particular task] in my class'. And this may, in itself, be true. When a child goes into a new environment his whole new 'theorising' about life begins again and he/she needs to experiment in the new environment because some or all of the variables have changed. Furthermore, each child with autism may see different aspects of the same event (as indeed we all do). It is helpful, therefore, at the beginning of a session to formulate a plan for the child so that he/she is able to implement and test the plan for him/herself. In this way children not only have a framework to follow but also a clearly defined beginning and end to the exercise. A lesson plan would need to include unfinished statements such as: 'I am trying to find out . . . I think this will happen . . .'. It would also need to structure the task for the child, hence it would need to include space for the pupil to list: 'what I need to collect before I start . . . what I need to do . . .'. Following each of these latter statements, numbered blank spaces for the pupil's response help further direct his/her planning. Evaluation too is important and such a plan ought to include space for a response to statements such as 'I liked this experiment . . . I didn't like this experiment' (making use of smiley/sad faces perhaps). This topic of evaluation is returned to later in the chapter.

## Experiencing self

Jordan and Powell (1995) write that 'a key difficulty in information processing in autism is a failure to develop and utilise an experiencing self', and that, therefore, pupils need to be helped to work at recognising their own involvement, 'without such recognition subsequent development of usable or flexible memories will not occur'. They talk of the development of a personal memory for episodes. Any difficulty in developing such a memory would have significant implications for the teaching of science. Videos and photographs should be taken while pupils are engaged in scientific activities so that when they come to analyse and draw conclusions there is visual evidence of their personal involvement. Photographs and videos are also useful in reminding pupils that they were successful in achieving a skill in a previous class or at a previous time; this can give them the confidence to try again. A summative file of Records of Achievement are beneficial in a similar way.

A series of photographs can be used to help sequence actions in a particular session for a particular child. For example it is helpful to provide reminders of the sequence within each particular task so that the pupil can see what he/she needs to do in order to go on to the next stage. Similarly this can be repeated if asking the child to recall experience. Such an exercise can also help with prediction, e.g. 'Which photograph do you think comes next?'. 'Here you are planting your plant. What did you do next?', and so on. It is helpful if you wish to recall an activity immediately after an event or lesson to have to hand a Polaroid camera so that immediate recall can be effected. In the same way, if a child is being asked to monitor an experiment over several weeks (e.g. growth of a plant), it is helpful if a photograph is taken at each stage so that the child is able to sequence the events.

## Executive function

Executive functions can be described as the ability to maintain appropriate problem solving sets for attainment of a future goal. Planning, impulse control, intuition of irrelevant responses help us maintain our organisational research. Recent studies (Jarrold et al., 1994) have looked at the ability of children with autism to plan thoughts systematically. It appears, these children performed poorly on tasks which involved executive function and hence planning. It, therefore, seems to follow that they will also have difficulty in any problem solving situation.

## Central coherence

Frith (1989) has commented on the preoccupation of some children with autism on focusing for a long time on a narrow section of a topic, almost for its own appeal, and not be able to focus on the whole topic. She also writes that children with autism may ignore the picture on a jigsaw but focus on the shape of individual pieces in the completed puzzle. If children are unable to see the whole picture of any construction, event, or illustration it seems to follow that they will have difficulty making sense of any new situation. In order to solve a problem in effect one needs to assemble all the separate facets of the situation to be able to reach a conclusion or solution. Following on from this it would seem that children with autism see concepts in terms of fragmented parts of the whole. If this is the case they will have great difficulty assembling the constituent parts and seeing a task, skill or event as a complete entity. Indeed structuring a situation in a more formal way may ultimately lead to children being more flexible and their thoughts more organised.

Implications for teaching of a central coherence 'deficit' can be summarised as follows:

- Sometimes it is useful to list the parts of a session for children who can read so that they are able to follow separate parts as they happen. In this way children with autism are able to see a beginning and an end to a session and begin to recognise progression and sequencing.
- For children who are unable to read presenting a lesson so that each stage has a visual clue is helpful. Cartoon strips can also be useful with empty speech balloons for the children to add the steps of the activity. Tasks can be presented as a series of photographs or line drawings. One task could be for children to sequence a series of photographs themselves. Describe simply each stage so that the child knows exactly what is expected.
- Sometimes a lesson may require a child to make an 'end product'. It may be necessary to present 'one I made earlier' so that children have the example as a point of reference.
- It may be useful to present the 'whole' concept at the beginning of several sessions and teach to each part as time progresses. If you want the child to follow the life cycle of say a chicken or frog have the sequence of pictures ready to hand e.g. a hen laying an egg, the egg in an incubator or the hen sitting on the egg, chick hatching, newly hatched chick, and so on. Show the child at each stage which picture you are talking about at each session. This may be against the practice of many science teachers who prefer the pupil to assemble and discover a solution entirely themselves. However, for children with autism such prompts may be essential if they are to persevere and see that there is a desired goal. An incubator can be hired so the children can watch the eggs actually hatch, feed the chicks and monitor their growth. Similar sessions can be facilitated to enable the children to catch frog spawn, watch its development, chart growth, release the frogs, etc.
- Some children find checklists useful so they can be sure that they have completed all the activities necessary or all that is required of them.

Teaching children to assemble or integrate all the parts of the event into the whole may permit the solution to a given problem and be more likely to lead to more confidence the next time a task is attempted. Some children are able to formulate their own checklists and so become more responsible for their own learning.

- In any science lesson it is helpful if children are enabled to record the result of any project at each stage as results are known. In this way they are able to retrieve results more effectively when they come to do so at the end of the project.
- Prompts or suggestion cards can also be used to help a child to go on to the next stage. Sometimes it is helpful if the child has to pick one from three in a multiple choice selection.
- If a child is unable to start a task because he is unable to collect all the necessary items together a card could be provided to help the child to focus on the materials he needs or what to do first. Eliminating the social aspect of teaching sometimes helps the child with autism to concentrate more effectively. The written word, visual prompts and the use of economic language are ways to reduce unnecessary distraction.

## Developing Scientific Skills

### Developing organisational skills

Children with autism usually love routine and predictability. The TEACCH programme (Watson, 1985) has focused on the effective use of these 'strengths' along with a strong emphasis on a visual approach to learning. It helps children to organise themselves effectively and can be adapted to be extremely useful when teaching science. Care must be taken, however, that children do not become too reliant on this approach and, in my own view, teachers must be proactive in encouraging flexibility. However, structure can facilitate flexibility. Visual plans, step by step teaching can encourage independence however directed the system in the first instance appears.

If a child has poor sequential memory and poor auditory processing we cannot expect him/her to retain a series of instructions throughout the carrying out of an experiment for example. We would not dream of instructing a hearing impaired child by means of masses of spoken language. Why then expect a child with poor auditory processing to do any better? Children can be introduced to problem solving activities in a framework of security given the right circumstances. The needs of each pupil with autism must be individually assessed and planned for within an individual education plan even when working within a group.

Questions teachers need to ask of themselves in any science lesson are as follows:

- Do children know what is expected of them? (Are you sure?)
- Do they know where to find things?
- Are necessary materials etc. accessible?
- Are items labelled?
- Are shelves labelled?
- Do children know what to do when they have finished? (At the bottom of the prompt sheet they may need an instruction to tell them.)
- Have you presented task visually for those pupils who need it?
- Do children know where it is safe to work? Have you told them?
- Are children organised enough to enable them to solve problems.
- Can children cross each instruction off as it is accomplished?

## Developing prediction

Children with autism find it difficult to predict – a skill which is almost essential in any science programme. Activities which can help the child to learn the concept of prediction can be taught in other lessons such as English but this is something that will have to be worked on at length and may have to be taught directly. Some helpful strategies are as follows:

- When playing board games or language games try to ask 'Who do you think will win? Sarah? John?'.
- Hide and seek game 'Where do you think Sarah is hiding'. 'Were we right or wrong?'. 'Was she in the cupboard? Under the table?', etc.
- One child hides behind a screen. Another child or the teacher describes simply what the child is wearing. The first child has to guess who it is. The teacher may also give a description of a child saying 'He is a boy, he wears glasses, who is it?'. 'Were we right, was it Tom?'. 'Yes it is Tom'.
- During the telling of a story ask children to predict the end e.g. 'What do you think will happen to the train?', Sometimes it is helpful to give alternative endings and ask the child to choose one of them.
- Children dress up behind a screen One child is given two costumes (say policeman and doctor). Another child is on the other side of the screen with a helper. The child who is guessing is asked, 'Is David going to be a doctor this time or a policeman?'. 'Were we right or wrong?'.
- Ask children what they think will be for dinner, curry or sausages? 'Were we right? Who was right? Who said curry? 'Who said sausages?'.
- Chart the answers visually.
- Show a well known video, freeze a frame and try to get the child to

anticipate: What will happen next? What will happen if.? What could she do? Where will he go?

(n.b. Children with autism may need time to process information before making a response. Additional 'wordy' prompting may confuse and delay the response even further. Knowing the particular characteristics of the child will help assess the situation.)

### Developing an understanding of cause and effect

Children with autism may not understand the processes of an experiment or even the concept of cause and effect. It is helpful to use everyday situations to show children that one activity can have some bearing or effect on another. For example: playtime follows snack time; swimming means locating your towel/costume; blowing through a straw can make bubbles in soapy water; bouncing a ball harder makes it travel higher; raining outside means indoor play. In the same way, simple experiments demonstrating to children how substances change can be structured in science. For example, children can be given experiences of cause and effect by simple experiments. For an experiment to test water on different substances the teacher may only be wanting to show that properties can change. For an experiment to test the effect of water on different substances the teacher would need to have a range of materials easily accessible and available. Again you may need to prepare a prompt card or checklist for the child to collect all relevant materials. Where the child is unable to read, then photographs may be used. It is important that the child is able to tick off items for themselves.

For many children the actual materials will have to be readily available around the room. The assembly of the materials will be a major problem solving exercise in itself for some children with autism and may be the teacher's main aim. Very precise and 'unwordy' instructions need to be formulated so that the child observes the change while, for example, the water dribbles on each saucer. The child will need to be asked questions and data will need to be recorded at each stage to gain the appropriate comments. It is far easier for the child to remember each stage of the experiment in this way.

## Developing Research Skills

### Action research

Action research is a useful mode within which children with autism may become more involved in their own learning. It is a method which relies on personal research and usually involves the solving of a problem or proving a theory. Pupils may be given statements that they have to prove or refute and thus with help from adults children set out around the school or the local environment to ask questions and prove the statement right or wrong. Statements are given to children such as: three children in this class have black hair. Is this true? All fruit has pips. All teachers in this school eat meat. All plants need water to live. All of the trees in our garden are chestnuts. An ice cube from the fridge takes half-an-hour to melt.

Interviews can be prearranged prior to these sessions so that school staff and other children are prepared. Simple charts, prompt cards, clip boards can be taken so that children are able to ask predetermined questions that they may have prepared in an English lesson. Simple data sheets can be formulated so that children need only put a tick or cross next to the required answer. An ink pad and stamp can be used in a similar way for those who are poorly co-ordinated. Tape recorders can be useful here to emphasise the 'speaker-listener' roles and the physical use of the microphone will help with turn taking. When directing the children around the school to interview people about their families, their eating habits, their pets etc. it is helpful if the rooms in which the people are to be located have a photograph of the person on the door so that the children are able to check with an identical photograph of the person they have been given previously. The kind of whole school topics that are commonplace in education today (e.g. 'Myself', 'People', 'Our School'), can be researched in this way. Each activity can be differentiated for particular pupils and data can be brought back to the classroom and analysed accordingly.

## Topics and projects

It is useful to operate a topic/project system so that each class group covers the same topic but at different levels. In this way we can ensure that each child covers aspects of a topic but again at different levels as they move up the school. It may be essential for some children with autism to re-learn specific portions of any topic but this method does ensure that children do not receive the same material each year. Again, photographs and videos can remind children of previous learning. Topics can change half termly or termly. In this way children can explore scientific concepts in small groups or individually and differentiated activities should cater for all children. Educational visits related to the topic can be undertaken to reinforce and widen scientific experiences.

Topics are also useful for enabling children to experience many different subjects emanating from one theme and for children with autism this is extremely important. Many educationalists see the 'thematic approach' as being only useful for children during the primary years. However, for children with autism it is one way of linking all subjects around one theme throughout all ages, so long as the activities are age appropriate. By overtly linking History, Science, Maths, English, etc. children with autism may begin to make sense of their world and a whole picture of a topic is built from the constituent parts and events.

Environmental science can be introduced in this way so that children of all abilities and ages begin to look at the world around them in a practical way. Educational visits can also be arranged so that children experience at first hand the topic they are working on. Teaching children with autism in context has always been seen as an effective approach to learning.

**Educational visits**

It is important that before embarking on any visit of this kind that children are involved in their own personal research at whatever level it may be. In order to cater for a range of ability and behaviour there is a need for a high degree of organisation. Carefully designed work sheets, deployment of staff and resources are all important. Children with autism will need structure of their own and may need their own individual plan or timetable. The aim of the activity for each child should be known to all helpers before setting out. One child may be interviewing, one may be collecting objects, another may be classifying and so on. Differentiation of activities is paramount for success. Groups that are too large with few staff result only in crowd control and very little learning. A place can be visited several times and videos shown to the children of themselves there the previous time to remind them of the venue. Each visit then could have a different aim so as the total project becomes much more meaningful. A video can be made prior to the visit so that on the way to a venue children can recognise relevant features as they travel, although it has to be said, most children with autism tend to be astute at recognising the geography of journeys from quite a young age.

People such as local shopkeepers, park rangers, farmers and school staff can all be interviewed in order to help children learn how to collect information. Children can be asked to collect items in the local area and group them on their return. Classifying items can be facilitated by asking children to sort items to certain criteria e.g. things that are: rough, smooth, shiny, glass, metal. Displaying and labelling the materials they have classified will help the children's awareness and recall. Recycling projects are useful here and children with autism derive much satisfaction from sorting items and then taking them to the relevant recycling bins.

An educational visit in science could be planned as follows:

*Preparation for the visit*

- If possible it is helpful if a video can be shown of the place you intend to visit.
- A member of staff could go before hand and take photographs or bring brochures to show everyone.
  - Find out if anyone has been to the venue before.
  - Discuss expectations.
  - List order of events.
  - Prepare clipboards – some pupils can use the computer for this purpose.
  - Prepare interviews for certain pupils.
  - Practise interviewing techniques.

*During the visit itself*

- Listen to guide, at venue.
- Ask prepared questions.
  - Answer questions on clipboards, use ticks crosses.
  - Tape some interviews with staff/helpers at venue (make sure you have organised this first).
  - Take a video of the entire visit making sure each child is filmed doing or watching a specific activity. Photograph children during their involvement in an activity, this will help with memory afterwards.
  - Refer to visual order of events to ensure pupils are aware of the passage of time and start/finish.

*Follow-up to the visit*

- Talk about experiences relating to photographs.
  - Write about visit.
  - Listen to tapes interviews.
  - Show video – freeze frame when individual pupils are in evidence. Highlight what they are doing at that point.
  - Report back to another group who haven't been on the visit.
  - Prepare graphs and tables on the computer using data collected.
  - Read an account of the visit to an audience.
  - List the new things you saw that you haven't seen before.
  - Talk about souvenirs, materials that have been collected.

*Evaluation*

In autism the evaluation stage needs particular attention.

- What did you like best? Did you like the . . .?
- Did we get there on time? What time was it when we got there?
  - –Did everyone have a packed lunch/drink? What did you have on your packed lunch David? Did you have sandwiches, a drink etc.?
  - –Evaluate each others behaviour (own and others).
  - –Were there enough toilets?
  - –Was there an ice-cream van?
  - –Did you have to queue for an ice-cream?
  - –Was it a long/short queue?
  - –Did it sell the ice-cream that you wanted to buy etc.?

## Developing problem solving skills

Once routines have been successfully established and the child is secure within them it may be possible to attempt to develop ways of enabling the child to respond to pre-determined 'hic-ups'. These situations can be engineered in other lessons but have direct relevance to teaching problem solving strategies usable in science. Children with autism will need to be directly taught ways in which to seek help from others either by signing, symbols or language so that success is guaranteed. Situations can be varied in order to facilitate flexibility of thought and extend understanding. Teachers should not attempt this strategy until they feel the child is able to cope otherwise confusion and anxiety may result.

Kiernan, Reid and Goldbart (1987) suggest the following strategies are useful in developing these skills:

*Sabotage*: equipment can be deliberately modified so as to lead to unpredictability and thus children having to decide on a solution, e.g. giving the child 'dried up' felt tips to draw a picture.
*Error*: doing something incorrectly, e.g. the teacher does something obviously incorrectly like asking the child to brush his/her hair with a fork.
*Omission*: not doing something students have learned to expect will always be done, e.g. in setting the table omit to provide a dessert spoon for the targeted child.
*Choice*: offering alternatives; children may only be able to work from a limited choice at first; giving too many alternatives only confuses; offer, e.g., a drink of orange or blackcurrant.

When initially teaching in this way it may be that some children may not identify that there is a problem or will perhaps give up on solving a difficult situation. Careful preparation, a knowledge of the child and pitching a problem at the correct level are all important. Taking a child gently through each stage of a solution is also a pre-requisite to success. Staff need to be aware that correct responses may need to be modelled in initial stages of the programme. Some children may need to be given alternative visual prompts to help them decide on the correct solution. If a knife is missing from a table setting, a verbal or visual prompt could be set up, for example, they are asked the question 'What do you need?' and given limited alternatives from which to choose.

## Developing recording skills

Methods of recording data can begin at an early stage with children with autism and can be used in all subjects including science. Young children can be taken outside the classroom to the garden and every time they observe say a bird use a rubber stamp with a picture of a bird on it to record their observations. Early on children can be encouraged to make simple recordings of things that are known to them and initially try to include themselves as part of the representation (for example a series of photographs of children in the class with corresponding names above).

Charts can be developed whereby something (e.g. liking for a particular drink) is attributed to each child. In this example pictures of children would be matched with pictures of 'favourite' drinks. Simple representations of information collected round the school can be charted in this way. Colour of eyes, hair, skin, who eats a healthy breakfast, how many wear spectacles, who has the biggest hand span can all be shown in similar ways.

Communicating successes and results will be difficult for some children with autism. One way to help is by asking children to write down the stages of their activity and read these to others in the class. Children with autism may be able to list the actual events but are less likely to be able to answer 'why' questions. Showing others their results in the form of graphs, tables, pictures and models will help with this process.

## Developing evaluation skills

Children with autism may have difficulty with evaluation. At all levels the language of evaluation may have to be specifically taught. Like, dislike, want, reject are all concepts that are difficult to teach. Modelling again is useful and some science lessons can be based around the teacher tasting things and showing like/dislike and subsequently the pupil repeating the activity. Teachers need to ask questions such as: 'Why did you like the jam? Because it was sweet? Because it was red? Because it was smooth?'. Children may need a range of choices or options to help them answer a question and so develop their ability to reason. It is also helpful to the child if experiences can be written down as a list in order to help clarify a sequence of recent events, observations or experiences. Also, pictorial representations which can be made of the results using photographs, block graphs and charts will help the child's understanding. School assemblies are a useful medium for developing evaluation skills. Two classes can be given similar tasks to do and the results can be evaluated and compared. Reporting skills can also be developed here as children are able to report to an audience.

Evaluation sheets of various kinds can be used. For example, following plant growing experience:

| Name | Evaluation | Smiley/Sad faces | Photograph |
| --- | --- | --- | --- |
| Sally | Liked working with Tom | happy | |
| Ben | Ben's plant didn't grow | sad | |
| Tom | Toms plant grew the most | happy | |
| Sarah | Asked the questions | happy | |
| Ian | watered his plant daily | happy | |

Records of achievement can be given to children to record skills they have completed successfully. A summative file of records of achievement can be a useful and enjoyable way of enabling children to remember activities and their role in them. Children can also be asked to evaluate their own and others' performance in other lessons. Evaluating a performance in assembly, scoring each others activities in the gym (a forward roll for example) can be useful ways of encouraging assessment. Tasting their own and others' home made cakes, inviting each other and evaluating a meal they have made can also be useful.

Children can also be asked to evaluate whether they thought an experiment was a fair test. Usually, children with autism are able to understand fair and unfair in a limited way. It may be that the list of instructions around the experiment may have to be seen as 'rules' and breaking of any of the 'rules' may be explained as 'unfair'.

At the beginning of a session prediction, as we have seen, is important. Subsequently, evaluation at the end is equally important. Questions can be asked such as: 'Was this easy?'. 'Could you have added more water?'. 'Did you like the experiment?'. Children can also evaluate their own performance by developing self evaluation sheets. Many children will have to be helped to complete this process. Such self evaluation sheets need to contain unfinished statements; for example: 'The challenge was . . .'. 'My idea was . . .'. 'I used the following materials . . .' 'My result was . . .'. Each self-evaluation can be summarised with smiley and sad faces. There is also a place for more directive self-evaluations, such as a simple ticklist in which the following questions are asked: Did your plant grow? Did anyone help you? Did you enjoy the experiment? Did you ask questions? Did you interview anyone? Did you work in a group? Did you talk to anyone? Information Technology is a medium that can be used effectively here and programmes can be developed at an early stage to record results effectively.

## Conclusion

Generalising skills and teaching in context has for many years been a central issue in teaching children with autism. Allowing a child to plan an activity, be involved in and record progress while in the process of 'doing' seems to be a successful route in enabling children to develop a more effective memory and way of learning. The use of videos, photographs, graphic representation, lists, checklists, suggestion lists all help to prompt the child to the next stage of an activity. Planning any event can then become a daily activity.

Structuring the social aspect of investigation by keeping interview techniques simple and reducing language to actual communicative intent helps children with autism to eliminate non-useful or redundant language.

In science as in other subject areas, helping children with autism to be involved in their own learning (e.g.) by enabling prediction, the reporting of results and the evaluation of data, will hopefully enable them to function more effectively and in similar ways to their non-autistic peers.

## References

Claxton, G. (1984) *Live and Learn.* London: Harper & Row.

Frith, U. (1989) *Autism: Explaining the Enigma.* Oxford: Blackwell.

Jarrold, C., Smith, P.K., Boucher, J. And Harris, P (1994) 'Comprehension of pretense in children with autism'. *Journal of Autism and Developmental Disorders,* **24**, 433–455.

Jordan, R. R. Powell, S. D. (1995) *Understanding and Teaching Children with Autism.* Chichester: Wiley.

Kelly, G. (1955) *The Psychology of Personal Constructs, Vols I and 2.* New York: Norton.

Watson, L.R. (1985) 'The TEACCH Communication Curriculum', in E. Schopler & G. Mesibov (eds) *Communication Problems in Autism*. New York: Plenum Press.

## COMMENTARY

## Individuals with Autism as Independent Learners

As Maddock points out 'doing science' involves a number of thinking skills that present difficulties for children with autism. For example, *predicting* is given high status in current notions of a science curriculum in the UK and being able to predict involves moving beyond the information given – something which children with autism find difficult. So, it may seem that Maddock is faced with a considerable challenge when trying to discuss a science curriculum in autism.

She starts by making the important point that learning facts and skills in science is not enough; teachers also need to try to ensure that children are, wherever possible, in charge of their own learning. This point recurs through many of the contributions in this book. All contributors allude, in one way or another, to the need to go beyond the delivery of curriculum products in the form of knowledge and skills to a notion of using the curriculum as a vehicle for the improvement of the child's abilities independently to understand the world and his/her place in it and to communicate that understanding to others. Science within this conception becomes, as Maddock suggests, a 'medium which promotes communication, allows problem-solving'. Indeed, science can be interpreted as a productive medium where the essence of 'ways of looking at the world' can be distilled and taught.

## Individuals with Autism: Objective Non-Scientists?

Maddock suggests that the non-autistic are continuous problem solvers, forever hypothesising and experimenting to try out new ways of understanding environments, relationships and so on. And she points out that such processing is not typical of the autistic way of living in the world. So, in autism we find individuals who do not behave in the way in which we are told that scientists behave. Yet we also know that those with autism are objective beings and objectivity would seem to be a key scientific characteristic.

Clearly, what is needed then is an approach in which the liking for structure and the strength in objective thinking are employed to create effective learning situations. Maddock shows us how to create a structure that will enable the child to work through a task in an experimental context. By setting down what 'I am trying to find out', etc. the child is enabled to focus on the task and maintain that focus throughout. In turn, the evaluation is given a clear structure which includes the requirement that the pupil respond to the question of whether or not they 'liked' the task. In including this as a planned part of the task Maddock is recognising the importance of evaluative appraisal in learning. Again, this is something that children with autism find difficult but it is also something that they need to do if future recall and use of current learning is to be effective and it is something that they *can* do given an appropriate learning structure.

## A Special Curriculum or Just Good Practice ?

Considering the *Pupil Plan* that Maddock suggests it is clear that this plan would be a perfectly acceptable part of the planning for a non-autistic child's experience of learning about science. Indeed, this is true of much 'good practice' in autism: what is helpful for those with autism will usually be of help to the non-autistic. The question may therefore be raised: 'are we then talking about good teaching as good enough for those with autism?'. The answer to this must be, in part, no. What the child with autism requires is a different focus, and the same materials may be employed in a different way to this end.

There is a sense in which the non-autistic child will evaluate whether or not they have enjoyed the task and they will use this evaluation to make the learning more effective in a future scenario whereas the child with autism will not. That is not to suggest that such children might not enjoy (or might not dislike) science tasks but rather that their feeling about doing such tasks does not 'step up' into being an evaluative appraisal. They need a structure, such as the simple ones suggested by Maddock, if they are to do this.

## Experiencing Self

Maddock gives some good examples of how to use photographs and video to help children with the reflection part of the learning cycle, and she highlights the fact that the power of visual records of activities for children with autism should not be underestimated. It is important to remember what was discussed in the opening chapters: that the autistic kind of memory processing does not permit spontaneous memory search and that, therefore, a structure is needed that cues the autistic learner into the salient points. Once that initial cueing has taken place the pupil may well be able to operate effectively. Associated memories are likely to be more readily accessible once that initial cueing has taken place.

## Presenting the Whole at the Outset

Maddock suggests that teachers of science generally may wish pupils to 'assemble and discover' solutions to problems for themselves. Certainly this would fit with much of the rhetoric of science education. Inevitably, of course, there is some manipulation here. Pupils in schools 'discover' what the teacher has predetermined by his/her choice of activity; indeed if the pupil were to discover something different then he/she might well be judged to have got it wrong. So, when Maddock asks for presentation of the whole concept at the outset for those with autism she is asking for no more than simply a clearer structure within which the child can operate than might be necessary for the non-autistic. 'Discovery' then is a relative term. For the child with autism, to work through a series of sub-tasks in order to get to a situation predetermined by the teacher may well involve them in operating at their optimum level at a given point in time in terms of uncovering the nature of a concept.

# CHAPTER 6

# Dance and drama

Stephanie Lord

## Introduction

The implementation of an effective curriculum for pupils with autism, who display a diverse range of learning styles, makes it necessary for teachers and carers to think about a range of approaches that will be supportive and motivating and encourage children to take a more active role in managing their own actions. I have used dance and drama in my teaching, to provide a source of ideas to use as starting points and to address a number of communicative behaviours. Activities are chosen to develop body and self-awareness, joint attention experiences and social interaction play which contribute to pupils sense of 'self' and awareness of 'others'. The processes involved are about helping children to make connections with 'who they are' and 'what they do' in their relationship with others.

It is not possible to offer a complete overview of the conventions, structures, and strategies used in these two art forms, but I have provided a selection of ideas that I have used and that have worked. Suggestions for other contacts appear at the end of this chapter and these may introduce the reader to new ideas or confirm the reader's own practice as a model that is appropriate to use.

The National Curriculum Council has emphasised that schools need to develop a more positive view of the arts in meeting special educational needs and promoting a broader concept of educational ability. Arts, defined as art, dance, drama, music and technology in the national curriculum, identify and develop the abilities of pupils that are not necessarily in the cognitive or intellectual domain (NCC, 1990). Value is placed on what children can do and on finding ways to support their development. By including arts subjects in the National Curriculum, creativity and the development of imagination are no longer viewed as innate qualities which are unattainable, but rather skills, subject to the influence of teaching.

Children with autism need to learn to create and be imaginative and by teaching and developing fundamental skills, which include symbolic understanding, children can be given the opportunity to rehearse and develop these in new and different situations. Creating and imagining can now be defined, at the initial stage, as doing something new differently. A necessary condition for being imaginative is to master a sense of self. This means significant emphasis should be placed on developing pupils' knowledge about themselves. OFSTED (1992) endorses this view by suggesting that the arts are considered within a framework that consists of creating and performing, and appreciating and appraising. Unfortunately, the guidance contained in the few sentences for dance (in PE) and drama (in English) provide little information on how to achieve this development with children with autism.

As subjects, dance and drama can be considered as umbrella terms which describe many activities for learning in a more dynamic form. Approaches that can be used are multi-sensory and aim to stimulate learning in a meaningful way within a social context that promotes decision and choice making. Planning for dance and drama is about selecting from a range of possibilities that include sensory stimulation, demonstration, imitation, commentary, role play, rehearsal and feedback. Both subjects draw on the other arts to enrich the process of learning, and in this way children's preferred modality for learning can be incorporated into chosen activities.

## Dance and Drama in a Context

### Aspects of the activities

'Dance' is used to describe movements that are performed for their own sake. Just as children need to learn to speak, sign, write and read in order to express themselves more fully, they need to learn how to create, perform and appreciate dances. By exploring movements children are able to develop a movement vocabulary for their own use. In developing this way of working, I have drawn on four types of movement approaches:

*Passive movement* is where adults feed in body sensations to enable children to gain a concept of 'physical self'. This can be in the form of touch, massage or the movements of their bodies in a caring relationship. Children's bodies can be held and rocked, limbs supported and lifted to experience a range of movement. At this stage children are not necessarily required to make a physical response, but over time the activities often promote the first stages of communication and social interaction.

Interactive massage can have a positive effect on reducing anxiety and stress levels by providing quiet times when demands for engagement are reduced. Touch is very important to the nervous system and any part of the body which does not receive normal tactile stimulation may develop a protective, as opposed to a discriminatory, response. The tendency to react negatively is termed 'tactile defensiveness' and a child with this problem may find many sensations uncomfortable. I have found that deep pressure in back massage or foot massage and increased vestibular stimulation by being pulled or rolled in a blanket, is more acceptable with this group of pupils.

*Functional movements* in the form of Sherborne Developmental Movement or yoga-exercise leads to improved co-ordination of the body and development of balance. These movement experiences help children gain an awareness of self and spatial awareness and provide opportunities for partner work. Development proceeds from the mobility patterns of supine flexion (lying on your back), prone extension (on your front), and rolling, to stability in weight bearing positions. In weight bearing positions, mobility and stability are combined in a sequence to encourage bilateral and unilateral activities. This progression can be observed when watching normally developing young children get up from a supine position. They roll over, push up onto elbows and hands to all fours and then either pivot to sit and pull up to a standing position from sitting, or pull up from all fours to a kneel-stand and then stand. Visualisation of this may be helpful in recalling the general sequence of motor development when observing pupils with developmental delay in order to plan appropriate activities.

*Expressive movements* take the form of movement phrases which link the rhythms and patterns made by the body with action, emotional vocabulary or rhymes. Expressive movements serve no practical purpose but reflect ideas, emotions and moods. I have found the use of materials and artefacts the most useful way of stimulating ideas for movement for children with autism as this offers an opportunity for pupils to extend their symbolic understanding by gradually replacing real objects with representation in pictures, photographs and words.

*Dance* involves improvisation to create simple characters, narrative or themes in movement. To create a dance there must be a clear beginning, middle and end to the sequence which can be repeated and modified in any number of new ways. The quality of the dance will depend entirely on the inner attitudes of the individual child at the time of making the movement. At this stage, awareness of others is gained in the making of group dances and sharing through performing. Watching and describing the actions of other children is an important part of identifying and clarifying the difference between the self and others. Dance is like describing poetry or music; it is expressed through phrases and sentences which can be repeated or added to. Laban analysis of movement (1948) provides a helpful framework of what children need to be able to do to make and participate in dance:

*Body awareness* is concerned with what we move. Each part of the body can initiate movements that meet, make contact and part.

*Spatial awareness* is concerned with where we move. Limbs can make patterns on the floor or in the air. The body can move forwards, sideways and backwards. Body actions can involve stretching up high or sinking low, reaching out to the side or curling around the body centre. Gestures invite relationships with other people. Movements can take place in personal space or move into general space.

*Dynamic awareness* is concerned with how we move. Movements can be sudden, quick as a flash, sustained and ongoing or so slow you hardly notice. They may involve muscular tension to be firm and strong or be delicate and light.

*Relationship awareness* puts a focus on who we move or dance with. This can be under the direction of an adult, in a partnership or group experience where adaptation, negotiation and commitment to others is necessary.

'Drama' can be described as a mode of learning in which children draw on their knowledge and experiences to create a fictional or make believe world. By participating in imagined roles or situations, children can be encouraged to question, think out loud, explore events and relationships by considering the actions, feelings opinions and viewpoints of others. Drama activities aim to stimulate responses from children without suggesting there is any one answer.

Perhaps the most important aspect of these activities for children with autism is the opportunity for involvement in relationships with their peers and teachers, that are non-judgemental because there is no right or wrong way to respond. In drama involvement is encouraged and supported rather than demanded. The achievement of sociability is often the most challenging demand placed on children.

Since children with autism will vary in their understanding of gesture, speech, and the ability to participate, activities will range from simple one to one games at a sensory motor level to activities where the child is encouraged to imitate and participate. Teaching targets that involve the development of early communication skills can be set in a context that is fun and motivating, combining several objectives in one game. Contexts that are related to real life experiences can be practised by more able children as an exploratory route to new knowledge and understanding, even though we may need to adopt specific strategies to generalise these skills to settings outside school.

Dramatic play follows a sequence of activities necessary to develop: awareness of the body, ability to copy and imitate, ability to make believe with objects, ability to make believe through action rhymes and simple role play, games to engage in make believe, and dramatisation of a fictional context to create potential areas of learning.

## Drama as a cross curricular theme

In planning drama as part of a cross curricular theme there are a number of structures that can be used to create learning opportunities regardless of ability. The following approaches are key and underpin much of successful drama activity:

*Teacher in role* is where the teacher, by talking to the pupils as if they were someone else, takes part along side them in creating the drama. It requires 'thinking on one's feet' as pupils responses and behaviour may present management challenges and many of them will find it difficult to sustain involvement without sensitive support. Idiosyncratic responses will need to be converted into ideas and initiatives that can be represented as learning experiences for the group.

*Mantle of the expert* is where the pupils are regarded as having special knowledge of the situation they find themselves in. In practical terms, this involves planning activities in a differentiated way to take account of different levels of conceptual and social development. Elements of cross curricular learning in PSE, history, geography, science or mathematics can be included in the drama so that something already experienced can be remembered and used in an imaginative context.

## Phases of a session

Phase one involves setting the context: the teacher invites the pupils to create a fictional context by asking specific questions to which there is no right or wrong answer. Everyone's suggestion is valued and views and wishes are respected.

*Selecting the topic*: From the planned curriculum? The teacher's ideas? The pupil's suggestion?

*Creating the place*: Where shall we work? Where shall we go? You choose?

*Establishing the roles*: Who can help me? Who knows what to do? Who would you like to work with?

*Deciding on the action*: What happens next? How can we make this work?

*Agreeing the time*: When is this taking place? Shall we start now?

Phase two involves developing the story: the purpose of this is to get the pupils involved in what happens in terms of the story and action. Children often become involved because the drama being created is of their own making and they can choose the level of their participation. The teacher moves the process forward by leading questions 'what happens next', 'who can show me what to do', 'why do you think that happened?' These can be used at a simplified level 'what next', 'show me', 'you do it'. Strategies for use include sound tracks, photographs and artefacts to create the atmosphere, meetings to discuss information, telephone conversations giving inside information and reporters who commentate on the action, even at a simple word level.

Phase three involves introducing a challenge: by introducing a challenge or problem, pupils have an opportunity to think aloud and share their ideas. All are accepted and considered by the group. Strategies to introduce a problem can include notices announcing a meeting or cancelling an event, headlines from a newspaper to focus on the problem to be explored, letters given to one person and artefacts that present a challenge to be explored.

Phase four involves reflecting and relating to reality: it is at this point the teacher tries to make firm links between what has been explored in the drama and the real world. It is the time when the teacher can check learning has taken place by spending time discussing the feelings that were evoked in the drama. This can also be achieved by the staff working with non-verbal students, commentating on their participation and bringing to their attention a significant moment in the drama.

## The Role of the Teacher

To use dance and drama activities effectively the teacher has to appreciate the emergent nature of the work. Teachers have to act as intermediaries in a negotiation process ensuring that the pupils have a chance to participate in partnership or group work. This is not a directive role, but one that encourages, supports and invites the pupil to join in. To be successful the teacher must be comfortable in this role. Developing the confidence of support staff by explaining the aims and objectives of the learning areas that it is anticipated will be covered, will help them take a positive role in empowering pupils, by facilitating opportunities for participation.

In order to do this, the teacher needs to analyse the content of each lesson, identify its component parts, and match these to the developmental level of the pupils. Knowledge of child development and the processes which underlie movement and social behaviour are important to remediate specific problems for particular groups of children. However, where investigation and experimentation are used, mistakes and failures may result and must be seen as part of the learning process. Positive praise and encouragement for participation is crucial in developing pupils' confidence.

# Difficulties Experienced by Children with Autism

Reports by Cesaroni and Garber (1991), based on their analysis of the first hand reports of people with autism, identify that it is important to recognise the strong need for human contact despite the unusual behaviours they displayed. This poses a dilemma as many children we teach seem to find being held or touched highly distressing and avoid contact wherever possible. There may be understandable reasons for this as unpredictable and uncontrolled human contact has been described as frightening and confusing by people with autism. There may also be underlying sensory and motor disturbance that contribute to the avoidance of personal contact.

Most children appear to have relatively mature walking and running patterns, but have immature patterns in bilateral movements. There is sometimes a discrepancy between the actions of the upper and lower limbs which cause problems in co-ordinating movements. A generalised lack of strength and poor timing, problems in retrieving sensory information, particularly kinaesthetic, add to problems experienced in relationship work. These observed differences in patterns of movement make it worth considering the inclusion of activities in the curriculum which generally enhance levels of development and specifically address some of the problems unique to autism.

Donnellan and Leary (1995) propose that we should consider and understand autism in terms of complex motor and movement differences in addition to the accepted triad of impairments. They point out that, although recognition of a problem will not automatically suggest ways to accommodate it, it allows us to consider changing teaching approaches and adjusting our interactional style. This view is very much supported by the work of Nind and Hewett (1994) who developed relationships through intensive interaction, based on styles reflecting relationship play with pupils with very challenging behaviour.

Both Temple Grandin (1992) and Donna Williams (1996) have described their difficulties in thinking and feeling and acknowledging the relationship between self and others. Williams suggests that it is the inability to simultaneously take account of self and others that is the cognitive problem which underpins most of the social and communication difficulties of people with autism. Grandin holds the view that lack of comforting tactile input is a major problem for most children with autism. She describes that as a child she longed to be touched but found these sensations painful. She wanted to be hugged and rocked but found the sensations overwhelming. Eventually she built a squeeze machine, similar to the type used to hold cattle, so she could experience the comforting feelings she craved for.

Grandin also suggests that her hyperactive behaviours, common in a number of children with autism, were due to high stress levels similar to being in a state of constant stage fright. The only way she found to control this was to engage in strenuous rhythmic exercises, or by co-ordinating her movements and synchronising her rhythm with someone else's. Two developmental areas can be distinguished that seem to have a significant effect on the ability to make relationships; these are abnormal responses to stimuli and abnormal synchrony in movement patterns.

Abnormal responses to stimuli include both touch and hearing. Reactions can vary from complete insensitivity to over-reaction at the slightest touch or attempt to interact. These perceived reactions to normal levels of stimulation lead to a range of behaviours which may be observed as panic attacks: high levels of anxiety, task avoidance, aggressive behaviour towards others and self-stimulatory behaviour. Research (Jones et al., 1995) indicates that over time responses to stimuli affects the way children relate to objects, events, and people, which ultimately leads to stereotyped behaviours.

Many adolescents with autism have developed postural abnormalities arising from tension held in the muscles of the neck, back and shoulders. Movements appear mechanical and superficial and are not generated from a body image that indicates they know how their body feels. Problems with muscle tone can give pupils an appearance of being floppy and weak and generally unresponsive to touch. Some pupils compensate for this by hyper-extending their joints and sitting or standing in odd positions. Low muscle tone also contributes to difficulty in maintaining postural stability and some children display a reluctance to sit or lie down which could be interpreted as being unco-operative.

Children with high muscle tone may develop constrictions around their joints and this leads to abnormal gait problems and restricted movements in the hip and shoulder girdles. If the body appears to be under abnormal tension, then the amount of feedback from the environment will probably only have a limited impact on the ability to learn new concepts. Disturbances in the kinaesthetic system may mean that children repeat the same action over and over again. The kinaesthetic system provides important information without reference to external receptors of vision and hearing and is now understood to be essential for the maintenance of posture, the control of muscle tone and the coding of movement memory which includes laterality and directionality, which in turn assists the learning of skilled movements (O'Brien and Hayes, 1995). These motor impairments could inhibit the learning of gestural communication and have consequences for symbolic functioning in dance and drama. We also know that diminished visual feedback is not uncommon in people with autism and this in itself will cause problems when required to imitate the actions of others in learning situations (DeMyer et al., 1972).

## What to Do in Practice

Although known about for some time, it is only recently that the use of Massage (Field, 1995 Longhorn, 1993; Sanderson and Harrison, 1992;), Conditioned Relaxation (Semuha, 1992), Yoga (Gunston, 1993), Developmental Movement (Sherborne, 1990) and Drama (Peter, 1994), to bring about a sense of self-awareness and control of complex behaviours, has been described. One of the aims of teaching massage and relaxation as a part of the movement and drama process is to produce a state of calmness where the muscles can start to relax, breathing becomes deeper and the body comes under the control of thought processes rather than being caught up in preservative action. Unnecessary tension causes discomfort which the child may or may not be aware of and as energy is being used to contract muscles, this can lead to distorted information processing via the sensory channels and subsequent loss of attention. The ability to relax, in order to participate in learning new skills, is an important goal. The ability to relax, sit and watch, while waiting for your turn in an activity or watching others share their work, is an essential part of group work.

Teaching relaxation and massage requires that one develop a basic kit which should include: symbols, photographs, materials, music, foam wedges, cushions or bean bags, paint brushes, body rollers, elastic exercise bands, foam balls. Initially, the teacher will need to structure the learning environment so that external stimuli are reduced. This may mean working in a plain room or space where superficial apparatus is removed. Children should be given their own personal space marked with a mat, blanket, towel or cushion. This can be moved around the room to establish personal space but still being within the group. Initially, activities should be introduced that are slow or performed to a steady rhythm, requiring just one response. Using squeeze toys and pairing the word *tight* and *relaxed* and similarly working with exercise bands while pairing the words *stretch* and *relaxed* are very useful.

Teaching breathing has a known effect on reducing anxiety states and this can be achieved through the use of blowing toys such as windmills, bubble blowers or straws in water. Initially pairing the words *blow* and *relax* can be extended when using yoga postures to saying *SHU* or *HUU* when lowering the arms from above the head. Or *HA* or *SHH* when pushing the hands out in front or to the side. Having a clear starting and finishing posture, such as relaxing with hands on knees or down by the side, is important for the development of imitation.

Group relaxation can take place in a number of settings providing a focus for the start or end of activities. Shaping or modelling the desired response may be necessary at first, but if all staff use the approach, then generalisation occurs very quickly. More able students may be able to move to the stage of auto suggestion repeating:

| | | |
|---|---|---|
| Hands on my knees | I relax my hands | Hands are relaxed |
| Feet on the floor | I relax my feet | Feet are relaxed |
| Head down | I relax my head | Head is relaxed |

Massage as a planned part of relaxation can be used during the dance and drama sessions. Some students will find it difficult to lie on their backs as they feel vulnerable and exposed and may continually lift their heads to see what is going on. Sherborne (1990) suggests that the degree of self-awareness and trust a child possesses is shown in their ability to trust their weight to the floor. I have found that some students prefer to lie on their stomach and I teach this position because it enables me to feed in back massage and, even if the pupil wants to lift their head up to look around, I can still stroke their back.

New age music (available in most health shops), created for relaxation or yoga, can be used for a range of movements that require light touch and a flowing quality. Theme tunes from TV programmes or the *Music for Pleasure* series provide snippets of music that can suggest a variety of ways of moving. Music from a variety of cultures introduces another dimension to movement experiences.

It is difficult to be prescriptive because individual children's responses will be different, but in general I have found that staff have often given up an approach before the student is either used to what is being presented or has an understanding of what is happening. The conventions listed in drama, actively promote choice and inclusion, and allow the student to choose the level and timing of their participation. Obviously, staff decisions need to be made about total non-involvement and sometimes more active encouragement may be required once the pupil has observed others taking part. This may need to be phased over a period of weeks.

The model set out on the following pages illustrates approaches I have used, drawn from practice across all phases. I have set my ideas out in a structure of developmental levels that move from the notion of the child as passive recipient to one of active participant. I hope these ideas will provide building blocks along with developing ideas of the structures used. It is important to make clear that I am not advocating a disjointed approach. Developing activities in dance and drama should be seen as a continuum in the context of enriching a topic based approach or linking cross curricular themes.

### Sensory Movement Phase

Activities emphasise tactile, kinaesthetic and vestibular stimulation to develop the sense of physical self, and rely on staff working closely as a team to create a shared experience.
Staff need to look for responses and respond to them.

### Perceptual Movement Phase

Activities at this level require the pupil to make an active contribution in order to develop a sense of initiative through the use of materials, action rhymes and simple role play.

### Affective Cognitive Movement Phase

Activities at this conceptual stage are more demanding and based on the notion of sharing experiences demanding co-operation, to understand relationships between self and others.

### Massage

*Tactile stimulation* using paint brushes, paint rollers, body brushes, loofa mitt, fabrics, wooden massagers, electric massagers, foot spa.

### Massage

*Self massage* 'how long is your arm, where does it stop/start?'
'Tap your head, stroke your face, pat your chest, rub your tummy, shake your hands, slap your legs, pound your bottom'.

### Massage

*Self massage* to release tension, rubbing stomach, squeezing neck and shoulders, thumb circles on arms, hands and feet, stroking forehead and cheeks.

*Human massage* using hugs, rubbing, squeezing – pressure to back and limbs.
*Body part massage* to back hands and feet using finger and thumb circles.
*Inanimate massage* wrapping and rolling in a blanket, sari, netting, on a lilo, foam mattress or crash mat.

*Partner work* tapping, cupping, rubbing, stroking, drumming, over broad surfaces of body, i.e. back, arms and legs, hands and feet.

*Inanimate massage* pulling a partner along in a blanket, rolling them on a lilo

Resting on a vibrating cushion, using shiatsu massager on limbs.

*Inanimate massage* carrying or swinging one pupil in a blanket or pulling them along the floor, working as a team.

### Relaxation

*Support:* cradling, rocking and moving in arms of adult. Resting on the floor, sitting on a chair, learning over a table, receiving back massage. Lying on tummy or side. Rubbing hands and feet, raising and lowering limbs. Tensing hands and feet – pair words, 'tight and relax'. Squeezing toys, sand, play dough with fingers and toes. Blowing party blowers, bubbles, pair words 'blow and relax.'

### Relaxation

*Imitation* reinforce 'sit and relax'. Raise arms above head. Raise leg off the ground – 'relax your arm/leg – that's relaxed.' Using stretch bands or thick elastic around arms or legs. 'stretch/relax, that's good I can see you're relaxing.' Shape the response if necessary. From standing or sitting – lift arms above head, lower them and say SHU or HU as you breath out. Push hands away from body centre, say HA or SHH

### Relaxation

*Auto suggestion:* 'Hands on my knees. I relax my hands, my hands are relaxed. Feet on the floor, I relax my feet, my feet are relaxed.' Partner work: trust games, balancing, rolling in pairs, rocking in threes, stepping over sleeping partner. Reinforce: sit and relax, stand and relax, walk at ease, easily breathing Visualisation: using real objects and pictures, clouds, calm sea, rag doll, wooden puppet. Using actions to images – ice cubes melting, a boat floating on the sea, floating balloons, clouds in the sky.

### Yoga Exercise

With an adult shaping the movement. Row the boat. Ring the bell. Stir the cake. Chop the wood. Wind in the trees. Snail curl – curled up on side or knees – sliding forward to full stretch. Snake – lying on tummy lifting head off floor Soldiers – strong posture in any direction. Puppet on a string – bending over from waist.

### Yoga Exercise

Using imitation and pictures. Seal walk – lying on tummy dragging body along floor. Cat stretch – rounding and arching back. Cat stalk – moving on hands and knees in long movements. Dog Stretch – weight on hands and feet pushing bottom to ceiling. Dog bounce – transferring weight on hands and feet.

### Yoga Exercise

Walking with a partner or in a group to create shapes. Wind in the trees – arms held to the side, bending from side to side from the waist. Crane dance – stand on one foot raising arms to the side. Mountain pose – standing as tall as possible. Floating balloons – rising up from the floor with arms opening and expanding.

and relaxing.
Superman – balance on
one knee or one foot,
leg and arm extended
in a long stretch.

Elephant stride –
walking alternately –
placing one hand on
the floor in front of
feet.

Tight rope walker –
balance on one foot,
leg and arms out to
side.

### Developmental Movement
*Body awareness*
floor based – with
adult support –
rolling, curling up,
hip shuffle, spinning
on bottom, crawling
on stomach, sitting, –
rubbing knees,
shaking, clapping
hands, stamping feet.
Walking – learning to
start and stop.
Partner work: holding
hands, rocking and
swaying. Curling up
and hugging knees.
Back to back pushing
to slide along. Rowing
holding hands. Face
to face rocking
holding shoulders,
rocking heads resting
on shoulders.

### Developmental Movement
*Body awareness*
Floor based – trunk
supported on
forearms or hands.
- sliding on stomach
  – pulling with arms.
- sliding on back
  pushing with feet.
- rolling and curling
  up.
Sitting:, or kneeling
arms above head,
out to the side,
folded across body.
Feet: stamping,
tapping, drumming,
soles of feet together,
legs extended,
weight on hands and
knees, squatting.
Group work: holding
hands in a circle –
swaying, rocking,
rolling backwards

### Developmental Movement
*Body awareness:*
problem solving.
through Partner
work/group work.
'Can you make a see-
saw from standing?
Back to back,
balancing partners
weight?
Holding hands to tie
a knot?
Make tunnels to go
under and bridges to
climb over? Make a
pile of people.
Rocking horses- four
people kneeling
One person
balancing across
backs, Jumping jack
in threes.
Two people
supporting a swing
with arms

### Movement and Dance ideas
*Following* join in
child's spontaneous
sounds and
movements, imitate,
repeat in
conversation, but
keep to simple
movement words.

### Movement and Dance ideas
*Flexible action chants
or songs*
The Farmers in his
Den
London Bridge is
Falling Down
The Grand Old Duke
of York
Hokey Cokey
Conga

### Movement and Dance ideas
*Known modern
dances and folk
dances.*
Using simple step
patterns.
Lambeth Walk, Gay
Gordons, Cha Cha,
Circassian Circle,
Line dancing,
marching songs.

*Commentary story or song* chant or sing using familiar songs or rhymes.

- rocking, rocking we are rocking
- this is the way we pat our knees
- touch, touch, touch your toes
- tickle, tickle Peter's toes.

*Mix action into short phrase or rhyme dances.* Here I am jumping jack, jumping forward and jumping back. Turning here, turning there, turning, turning everywhere. Old MacDonald had a farm – create animal shapes.

*Group actions* Mirror mirror on the wall Follow my leader – each student takes a turn, Add a commentary to actions to make a phrase to be repeated by others.

### Using Materials Instruments
ribbons, streamers and fans to wave. Rhyme: Round your arms round your legs, now you're caught in a spiders web.

### Using Materials and percussion instruments
balls, balloons, streamers, feathers, ribbons, to develop expressive movements and sounds. i.e. dab, flick, pat, swish, whoosh, swoosh, crack. Parachute or lycra cloth for locomotion activities. Ball of wool or string to pass round bodies or limbs – children get caught. Game: fishing for facts – body part pictures from magazines on cards. Fish out card and show an action to match the part.

### Using materials and percussion instruments
Patterns and pathways; use chalk, string, wood to make a pattern for a partner to follow. Haunted forest; use bodies to make shapes and material to drape, chosen children move in and out. Carnival parade: Brass band, clowns, horses, jugglers. Human xylophone – tap out sounds on body parts under direction of a conductor. Mill and grab – join with someone who wears the same colour as you.

### Drama – moving into make believe

Begin by sitting on the 'story carpet'
Props to support movement.
Whose shoes? tap shoes, ballet shoes, wellingtons, riding boots, flippers, high heels, bit boots, roller skates.
Whose hat?
Cowboys, Policeman, Clown
Special occasions, celebrations:
Weddings, Christmas, Ramadam, Chinese New year, Disco, Picnic. Types of shops: baker, green-grocer, toys, fish and chips, cafe.
Types of places: bowling alley, cinema, swimming pool, rollerskating rink.

### Drama moving into make believe

Begin by saying 'I'm pretending.'
Dressing up box con-taining a range of costumes. Magic Box containing treasures – chant 'Hand in feel around. Pull it out – what have you found?'
Pictures or taped sounds, producing movements to match. Games: Guess what job do they do? Brooms and wheelbarrow, fishing rod and net, stethoscope and bandages.
Who lives there? – creating homes, shed, barn, caravan.
How does it work?
What shall we take with us?

### Drama – moving into imagination

Link action to imag-ination, say 'when we were pretending just now.'
Matching pictures with actions.
Circles of feeling - over the moon, down in the dumps, jumping for joy, on top of the world,
Environmental sounds – producing ideas to develop into action airport, eurotunnel, TV programme. What happens next?
Witches hat, a letter, a bike lying on the floor
table set for tea, suitcase packed with clothes
Where does it come from?
What can we make from?

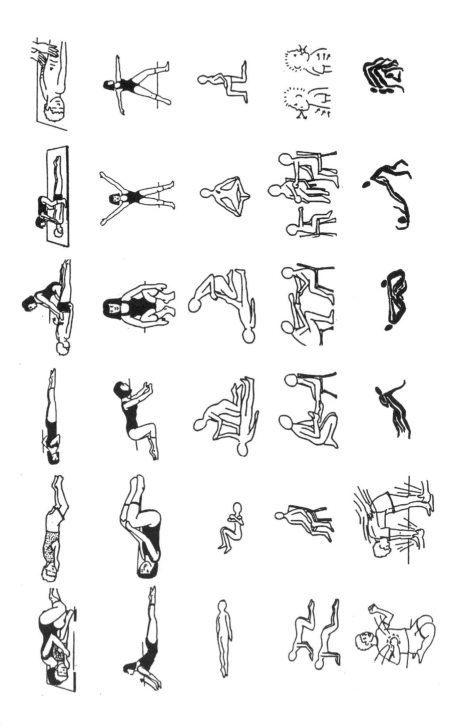

## Background Information for Training and Resources

*British Wheel of Yoga*, 1 Hamilton Place, Boston Road, Sleaford, Lincs NG34 7ES

*Connections: Interaction Through Movement*, Heathermount School, Devenish Road, Ascot, Berks SL5 9PG

Gunstone, M. *You and Me Yoga Centre*, The Cottage, Burton in Kendal, Carnforth, Lancashire LA6 1ND

*Laban Centre for Movement*, Laurie Grove, London SE14 6NH

*Sherborne Developmental Movement Centre*, Office No 5, Old School House,

Britannia Road, Kingswood, Bristol BS15 2DB

*Touchsound, Aromatherapy and Sound*, 3 Brookers Place, Chequers Street, Higham, Kent ME3 7JB

*The London Drama Centre* , The Holborn Centre for the Performing Arts, Three Cups Yard, Sandlands Street, London WC1R 4PZ

## References

Cesaroni, L. Garber, M. (1991) 'Exploring the experiences of autism through first hand accounts'. *Journal of Autism and Developmental Disorders,* **21**, 303–313.

DeMyer, M.K., Alpern, G.D., Barton, S., Demyer, W.E., Churchill, D.W., Hingten, J.N., Bryson, C.Q., Pontins, W. & Kimberlin, C. (1972) 'Imitation in autistic, early schizophrenic and non-psychotic subnormal children. *Journal of Autism and Childhood Schizophrenia,* **2**, 3, 264–287.

Donnellan, A. and Leary, M. (1995) *Movement Differences and Diversity in Autism and Mental Retardation. Appreciating and Accommodating to People with Communication and Behaviour Challenges*. Newmarket, Ontario: DRI Press.

Field, T. (1995) 'Massage therapy for infants and children'. *Developmental and Behavioural Paediatrics,* **16**, 2.

Grandin, T. (1992) 'An inside view of Autism', in E. Schopler and G. Mesibov (eds) *High Functioning Individuals with Autism*. New York: Plenum Press .

Gunston, M. (1993) *You and Me: Whole Body Movement*. Carnforth, Lancs: You and me Yoga Centre.

Jones, R., Walsh, P. and Sturmey, P. (1995) *Stereotyped Movement Disorders*. Chichester: Wiley.

Laban, R. (1948) *Modern Educational Dance*. London: MacDonald & Evans.

Longhorn, F. (1993) *Planning a multisensory Massage Programme for Very Special People*. ORCA Computers Ltd, Educational Services Unit, Neuhof, Luxenbourg.

Nind, M. and Hewett, D. (1994) *Access to Communication. Developing the Basics of Communication with People with Severe Learning Difficulties through Intensive Interaction*. London: David Fulton.

NCC (1990) *The National Curriculum Council Arts in Schools Project. The Arts 5-16 Practice and Provision*: London: Oliver and Boyd.

NCC (1992) *The National Curriculum and Pupils with Severe Learning Difficulties: INSET Resources*, York: NCC.

O'Brien, C. and Hayes, A. (1995) *Normal and Impaired Motor Development, Theory into Practice*. London: Chapman and Hall.

OFSTED (1992) *Framework for the Inspection of Schools*. London: OFSTED

Peter, M. (1994) *Drama for Alll: Developing Drama in the Curriculum with pupils with Special Educational Needs*: London: David Fulton.

Sanderson, H. & Harrison, J. (1992) *Aromatherapy and Massage for People with Learning Difficulties*. Lutterworth: Hands on Publishing.

Semuha, M. (1992) 'Conditioned relaxation'. *Communication*, **26**, 3.

Sherborne, V. (1990) *Developmental Movement for Children: Mainstream, Special Needs and Pre-School*. Cambridge: Cambridge University Press.

Williams, D. (1996) *Autism: An Inside Out Approach*. London: Jessica Kingsley

# COMMENTARY

## To Be Imaginative

One of the triad of impairments is often referred to as a 'lack of imagination', although we have preferred 'rigidity of thought and behaviour'. Certainly, when working with children with autism, teachers will often comment on the lack of imagination in these pupils. At a superficial level it is clear that in autism there are likely to be low levels of performance in areas of the curriculum which seemingly demand imagination and creativity such as the arts subjects. But the problem runs much deeper and has more wide ranging effects on learning. To be imaginative requires that an individual can extrapolate from one set of circumstances or stimuli to a different combination of elements or to a different context. To be able to perform such extrapolations requires the ability to explore the potentials in the original circumstance and this, in turn, requires the ability to manipulate mental models of things and people, etc. It also requires, as discussed in this chapter, a sense of self agency. Because of the difficulty in establishing a sense of self agency, as described in Chapter 1, individuals with autism will inevitably find it difficult to reflect on their actions and thus take them in new directions.

In one sense, therefore, it may seem that Lord's task, in discussing Dance and Drama as part of the curriculum in autism, is a difficult if not impossible one. Yet she shows how this area of the curriculum is rich in possibilities, not necessarily in terms of the production of art but rather in terms of activities that can be used to develop a greater sense of self and of other. She describes possibilities for learning about being imaginative. Just as Murray, in her chapter on IT shows that the computer context may enable the development of this sense of agency and then imagination, so Lord shows that the proximal senses of touch and movement may also offer a more fruitful route to this understanding by people with autism.

## The Child as Focus of the Curriculum

In common, once more, with Murray's chapter, Lord illustrates how, when dealing with pupils with autism, the child needs to be the focus of the curriculum. She also reinforces the views from the chapter on assessment, that the most valuable products of learning (the learning outcomes) are those that relate to improvements in the way in which the child is enabled to think of themselves in relation to others. These kinds of gain will have long-term effects on the child's abilities as a learner. One problem for the educationist, of course, is how to quantify this kind of gain. This becomes a serious issue when the system of education begins to value learning only if it can be measured or indeed value it in direct relationship to how readily it is measurable and again, that relates to the issues addressed on assessment.

Lord's chapter, is similar to others in putting forward the idea (obliquely in the case of Lord) that the teacher needs to start from 'where the child is'. If the child is defensive in tactile terms then Lord offers suggestions on to how to begin passive movement . If the child has difficulty with the part played by symbolic understanding in expressive movement then Lord suggests starting by gradually replacing real objects with representations in picture or photograph form. In each case there is acceptance (of the difficulty) and yet a desire to find a way of giving the child access to the desired learning. Indeed, as mentioned above, the learning outcomes themselves will need to recognise the particularities of the autistic style of learning. The purposes of the kind of curriculum that Lord describes are necessarily of a qualitatively different nature to those that might be set out for non-autistic children. This not to say that children with autism need a wholly different kind of curriculum to their non-autistic peers. What Lord shows is how children with autism need a curriculum that is adapted to their abilities and needs. She shows how the content might be universal but the focus within it for those with autism needs to be designed with their distinctive thinking style in mind.

## Curriculum 'Pace'

Here, there are echoes of Golding's description (in her chapter on group work) of observing and commenting on the activities of others, in the way in which Lord discusses gaining awareness of others through the 'making of group dances and sharing through performing'. Just as Murray suggests that a joint intense interest may represent the context for a more accessible form of commentary, so Lord suggests that joint movement may provide that context. Again, the important point is that this process should go on in the learning of the non-autistic within a dance curriculum; but in autism that process needs to be explicated overtly and at a pace that enables the child to learn. The notion of pace is important in autism. In previous writings we have employed the analogy of the dance to illustrate how the learner need to be involved in the process of learning by the teacher. We have suggested that learning to dance is very much a matter of learning how to adapt oneself to the pace of the movement of the partner. What facilitates such learning is clearly the rhythm of the music. In this actual (rather than analogical) situation of learning through dance, it seems clear from Lord's writing that rhythm acts as a structure which enables the pupil to begin to focus on the actions of others in a meaningful way. Indeed, we have often noted in our own work how children with autism are enabled to learn more effectively when rhythm is present in the presentation of material. For example, they may respond well to instructions which are sung to them or spoken in a sing-song voice rather than merely spoken (an observation which occurs again in the chapter on play). After all, we know that children with autism are able to use structure in their learning (we may even suggest that they are dependent on structure) and rhythm is simply a structure of sound (or indeed vision). In short, the kinds of success that Lord discusses may well highlight the necessity of structuring learning situations in autism – especially learning which is of the most difficult kind for them, namely social learning. And again, the kind of fear of physical contact that Lord describes (along with a paradoxical need for contact) is one which may derive in part from the unpredictability of human relations and contacts. Rhythm imposes a structure and, thereby, a predictability on such contacts.

An important point is made by Lord when discussing staff 'giving up' on a particular approach before the student has come to terms with it (in terms of learning). It does seem to be a theme running through a lot of analyses of teaching in autism that the time span between presentation of a stimulus, in whatever form, and the child learning to respond exceeds the kinds of teacher expectation of what is reasonable. It is not necessarily that teachers tend to be impatient but that their tendency is to look for ways of rephrasing or in some other way re-presenting the stimulus. Analyses of video often show a child being bombarded with well-intentioned rephrasing of instructions including new gestures or signs as well as re-organised language; the child may be just coming to terms with an instruction only to find it being changed for a 'better' one.

# CHAPTER 7

# Autism and information technology: therapy with computers

Dinah K.C. Murray

## Introduction

My concern in this chapter is with computers primarily as a therapeutic and secondarily as an educational resource. Their educational potential is very well recognised, and access to computer-assisted learning is becoming progressively more widespread (some access points are listed at the end of this chapter). It is also widely recognised that an element of therapy is essential in the education of children with autism (Jordan and Powell, 1995). The boundary is blurred. I suggest that the more directly educational potential may not be accessed, especially by non-verbal children, unless the calming, controllable, aspects of working with computers have first been explored freely. What is more, that phase of exploration and discovery can be an ideal basis for communication with a sensitive helper.

My central points are that anyone with autism, from pre-school age to adult, may be very comfortable with computers, and may relate happily with any knowledgeable companion who is focusing on the computer with them. Information technology offers scope to play, explore, be creative, in a safe, highly controllable environment – and it need not make any verbal demands. Computers can thus focus attention with minimal risk of overload. They may also provide various coping strategies for people with problems of self-awareness, information connection, and memory retrieval.

The method I recommend for maximising the value of information technology for those with autism is to sit beside one at the computer (not crowding!), with a graphics program running, watching every move they make. Do not intervene unless there is a call for it! Do not try to divert the flow! Do share joy or annoyance as they occur, and comment positively on what is happening! Do help if it is called for! The end result may be a much more confident and communicative child, whose openness will be of great help to the teacher.

# Why Computers Suit People with Autism So Well

Most of us most of the time have multiply divided attention: many interests simultaneously alert and ready to digest information – we have *polytropic interest systems* (Murray, 1995). In this way we cope relatively easily with a highly changeable environment while building up a richly connected information store. With autism, however, attention is tunnelled (Jordan and Powell, 1989), interest trapped: its objects isolated and without context – people with autism have *monotropic interest systems*. That makes for an alarming and unpredictable universe, and a fragmented, disconnected, information store to cope with it. (Readers can refer to the work of Courchesne, Frith, Happé and Jordan and Powell for arguments relating to attention and information processing in autism).

Many people find computers refreshing company. I believe this is true for steeply monotropic children, that there should be the earliest possible access to information technology for all children who have been diagnosed autistic. The list below highlights those features of computing which I think distinctively appeal to people with autism, whatever their age:

### Why computers suit autistic individuals

- Contained, very clear-cut boundary conditions.
- Naturally monotropic, (cf. Douglas Coupland's 'overfocused') thus context-free.
- Restricted stimuli in all sensory modalities.
- Rule-governed and predictable thus controllable (despite annoying mistakes).
- Safe error-making.
- Highly perfectible medium.
- Possibilities of non-verbal or verbal expression.
- Interacts *cotropically* with the individual, i.e. it *joins the individual's attention tunnel*, 'starts where the child is'.

## Contained, very Clear-cut Boundary Conditions

Few activities are as isolated from the constantly changing environment with its perpetually shifting and blurred distinctions as the activity of engaging with a computer. It offers a monotropic individual a strictly contained event receptacle. Everything which happens within that frame can be encompassed in a single attention-tunnel. It is a *naturally monotropic* medium: people who are normally relatively polytropic will tend to monotropism in front of a computer. This is the condition which Douglas Coupland calls 'over-focussed' in his very knowledgeable fictional accounts of life around Silicon Valley. But if a person is already in a monotropic state, working with a computer will simply reflect it, and by creating a state of relative ease will widen the attention window, not narrow it.

## Context-free

A corollary of that natural boundedness is that making sense of the information presented does not require accessing external context. Most of us non-autistic people automatically integrate information into a wider context and reel off ramified relevant inferences at all times (Murray, 1986; Sperber and Wilson,1986). It is something we have learned to do as the world has drawn us out. In our normal, flexible, polytropic state we can cope quite well with most of life's exigencies. Those perpetually occurring cognitive effects adjust relationships between interests in adaptation to the new. We are supremely context-sensitive beings. We can even handle modelling other people whose interests are distinct from our own: a vital skill for living in society.

I believe that many cognitive effects may occur in a person who is in a monotropic state, but they will not connect with information relevant to interests outside the current one. Therefore isolation from context is always a blessed clarification for someone with autism, who is chronically monotropic. Computers singularly have this virtue, as well as offering rich potential in cognitive effects. Understanding what's going on at any given moment requires no recourse to exotropic information, no effort at integration.

## Restricted Stimuli in all Sensory Modalities

Another aspect of computing's clear boundedness is that a strictly limited set of stimuli assails the senses. Most of the stimulus set remains stable: the hardware doesn't change; within its fixed frame, predictable events occur in a fixed order. Information is presented as minimally as representation will allow (because that is how to get maximum performance from a limited display). Change occurs within a very narrow range of sensory possibilities, usually one step at a time.

All the visual stimuli, including the peripheral (and also proprioceptive) information from hand and keyboard or mouse, seem to be manageable within a single attention tunnel. There is no need for redirection or readjustment beyond the cursor's movements, which are confirming the movements of the user's hands and fingers. It is a highly simplified and positively reinforcing universe.

## Rule-governed and Predictable thus Controllable

Computers provide access to their potential in a strictly rule-governed and highly reliable fashion (compared with events in the unrestricted universe outside). You can switch them off when you don't want them, or you can change their direction yourself. You can have complete control over your perceived environment. The many children with autism who find the normal lived environment overwhelmingly unpredictable and alarming tend to find all of these features of computing strongly appealing.

## Safe Error-making

Not only is the predictability of computers soothing, but they also provide a very safe environment for exploration. It is the rarest error which cannot be reversed, thanks to today's software, and frustrations can usually be overcome. In these very favourable conditions, autistic children seem entirely capable of imaginative play, play involving the not here-and-now, play involving the creation of new situations and the discovery of new methods.

The risks of such exploration are infinitely less in terms of exposure to shock and discomfort or serious accident, than the risks of real world exploration. For one thing, nobody is likely to misunderstand, or shout about mistakes (as they might have to in many cases of real world exploration). For another, the actual consequences of error-making on a computer are rarely worse than trivial, and can almost always be overwritten even when they cannot be undone.

## Highly Perfectible Medium

As well as providing ease of correction, computers also offer perfect forms to their users. As I write this, successive immaculate sans serif letters appear on the page – or I could find circles, polygons, stars, sprays, or whatever precise range of colours I chose from a huge visible array, if I switched to a graphic program. All of these can be had in flawless perfection in exchange for my perfunctory key strokes. Anyone can gain as much for as little pain.

## Possibilities of Non-verbal or Verbal Expression

Expression is an outward and perceptible sign of the interest or desire current at the moment of its appearance. On this definition, verbal expressions and other shared symbols are a special case of something more general and less formal. They are special in being fixed across millions of otherwise highly variable interest systems and they make very specific demands for the attention of their hearers. Once you have got used to speech, you have allowed your interest system to become structured by those aspects of the common culture which your language embodies. In normal discourse that leaves you wide open to having your interest system taken over by other people's words.

People with autism tend to find language invasively challenging behaviour, and not adopt it themselves as an expressive tool. Alternative means of expression will always be found. Non-verbal expressive behaviours can often be hard to accept for carers, or even physically hazardous. With Windows software it is possible to engage with a computer successfully entirely non-verbally, through icons. A great deal can be done, therefore, without encountering social/invasive problems in the symbolic realm. Even when access involves verbal items, being written rather than spoken, those items can be selected for attention at will. They do not impose in the same way as speech, do not peremptorily summon the attention.

## Cotropical Interaction

In effect, because it responds to every move you make and is guided solely by your choices, a computer itself behaves very much like the ideal human companion. It responds immediately but lets you take your time. Your interest dictates everything it does. What a great friend! There is a danger here that carers will let that apparent sufficiency justify leaving their charges in the 'care' of their computers, but no greater risk than there always is with anything which successfully occupies a child.

In this case, the object of interest is inherently interactive, so that the child is in effect taking turns with the computer, which reflects everything the child does. It can be fascinating to watch that process, and I reiterate that doing so and supplying help and/or an interested commentary can be an invaluable way to abet your relationship with that child.

## Risks

Is there not a basic danger that the computer will be so appealing to autistic individuals that they will become more autistic in relating to it? That is, both more obsessive and less interested in communicating with those around them? Firstly it should be borne in mind that in most situations nobody gets the chance to monopolise a computer. There is almost bound to be a need for turn-taking of the most basic kind, with other human beings, not just within the interaction between user and computer. Secondly, we are talking about naturally obsessive people when we discuss autism, they will single-mindedly do whatever it is they do. Thirdly, what they do on the computer obsessively may be highly creative and recognisably worthwhile – both to the person at work and to the observer. Fourthly, it can be so satisfying and generate such an easeful environment that it has a directly therapeutic effect in widening the individual's attention window. And fifthly – yet again – it can provide a fruitful basis for mutual communication, and the motivation to pursue it. Therefore it can make for a less severe autism, a more integrated person.

Ideally, every child with autism should have a definite period every school day during which she/he will get 1:1 support at the computer. Time will necessarily be limited and shared with others. Some shared activities, like games of various sorts can be timetabled. Children with autism are likely to be at least as good at most computer games as their non-autistic peers. Such games are not widely accepted as a suitable curricular activity. But the potential for peer group prestige, normalisation, and willing co-operation and communication is huge.

Some anecdotal observations from my own experience working at the computer with my autistic friend, Ferenc, and from that of Rosemarie and Les Mason, whose large family has profited greatly from its early exposure to information technology, will support these points.

Ferenc is a student at a special school for children with autism in North London, where he has been since he was six. He is classically autistic and has chosen not to go on using the limited spoken vocabulary he used to deploy (in both English and Hungarian) when I first met him as an 11 year old.

When the head of his special school, Bert Furze, urged me to befriend one of his pupils, it suited my own intentions very well – though I wasn't at all sure how to go about it. Happily in Ferenc I found someone whose interests I share. We both like nature, light, refraction and reflection, find beauty in them. We both like controlling material: making things, melting things, making sparks fly; we both relish the potential of computer graphics

I do a variety of things with Ferenc which give him the opportunity to take control – something he evidently finds satisfying. I try to provide a safe environment for him to explore. One of the most fulfilling activities for him has been time spent using fairly simple, but productive, graphic programs on a school computer. Because I had access to it – and perhaps also thanks to Nottingham's wonderful *A for Autism* animation – I introduced Ferenc to an animation program, when he was 14.

The first time we sat down to do an animation, I showed him a 16 frame one that my son had done. I played it through, then played it frame by frame, backwards and forwards. Ferenc watched with fascination. I asked him if he wanted to make an animation. He nodded with enthusiasm. So I explained what I had found out from my son about how to prepare to make a 'flic'. First you have to set a length by typing in a number: Ferenc reached across and keyed in '999999' until the space was filled up. I explained I thought the computer couldn't handle that, so we opted for 30 plus.

I sat and watched everything he did, as is usual in our encounters – he minds if I don't. Ferenc used a polygon facility which he knew from school, to make a green figure, placed differently in each successive frame. After 16 frames he paused and ran it through. It was a bit *too* animated, jumping unintelligibly from frame to frame. Without hesitation he carried on again, this time he kept the polygon rectangular and only slightly varying in size and took it on a journey round the edge of the screen, and then shrank it step by step and made it larger again. When he played it back, the rectangle marched smoothly round the border then angled off into the distance, then back. I said 'It looks to me as though it's going away and coming back again, is that how it looks to you?'. He gave me an emphatic nod.

On a later occasion, Ferenc spent some time learning from my son, both watching him doing things, and listening with apparent understanding to suggestions. Then I introduced him to my colleague Mike Lesser, who knows the program really well, and had the facilities for us to record everything Ferenc did on the computer, by downloading every screen onto video. Ferenc appeared to have a very good time round at Mike's. When I asked him a few weeks later if he liked Mike he affirmed it strongly. It took me a lot of intensive attention and care over a period of many months to build up the good relationship I have with Ferenc. But with the computer as a communication focus and motivator an excellent relationship was forged between him and Mike within minutes of their meeting. Mike knows how to show Ferenc aspects of the program he might otherwise miss, and can help him understand and control what's going on.

The first time, we successfully make two copies of his work, one for him, one for us, and he takes his home with him. That is unusual, since Ferenc will hardly ever agree to take anything home either from school or from when he's out with me. The second time, the technology isn't quite sorted: there is only one recording. I say, 'Oh, Ferenc, would it be all right if I took this home with me and gave it back to you on Monday morning?' (the day after the morrow). He shakes his head vigorously. Feeling very vexed (mainly with Mike), I grit my teeth and leave the room. Meanwhile, as I learn later, Mike goes up to Ferenc, who is holding the successful cassette, and eyeballs him with, 'Ferenc, you know Dinah really really wants it too. . .'. The next moment, Ferenc finds me in the kitchen. Clutching the cassette to him, he leans towards me, and makes an obviously strenuous attempt to extend the cassette in my direction. I say, 'Oh, is it all right then, if I take it home. . .?' He shakes his head as vigorously as ever. I shrug, and tell him never mind – resigned to never seeing it again.

Next time, we successfully (largely thanks to the help of Stuart Powell) set up a pair of recordings direct from the computer, plus an outside camcorder filming Ferenc himself, and our interactions with him. That was the session which resulted in the short video film we have made: *Working with Ferenc* (for a copy of this video, please apply directly to the author). When he has completed his animation, he gets up and goes to get Mike, and reaches out to shake Mike's extended hand when congratulated. At the end of that session, when I offer him his cassette, he refuses it, indicating that it is mine. I am very touched, as I am when he has pushed across the table towards me, the last four Ferrero Rochers (until then I'd had just one). Earlier, when I'd bought them, I'd asked him to remember that I like them too. It seems that he did remember.

Ferenc is far from being the only autistic person who shows creative imagination, pride in achievement, and a desire to communicate in relation to work on a computer. Rosemarie and Les Mason's youngest son, addressed his first words to a computer, during a game. He has gone on to talk quite fluently, and display all manner of computing skills. He has two autistic older brothers, too, one of whom has been an adept all along. The other one was the most extremely autistic member of the family, much given to tapping and banging, Sean.

There are three computers in play in this family of five (currently, aged between 6 and 11) and until recently, all the children except Sean were to some extent adepts. His parents thought of getting Sean a 'concept' keyboard – with minimal, large, key pads – or possibly a touch screen.

Then, when just turned seven, Sean went and got his mother and led her to a computer. She thought that he was wanting her to do something for her – since that had been the case on every previous occasion throughout his life. But in fact he pushed her aside when she began to grapple with the hardware, and showed her that he could access a graphic program with the mouse, that he could use the mouse competently – indeed, more competently than could she. He drew rainbows, appropriately coloured. Later he used the keyboard to type in numbers from 1 to 10. Away from the computer, soon after this breakthrough, Sean spontaneously began colouring in – something which had never occurred in him before

One night, when she thought they were all in bed, Rosemarie went upstairs and suddenly realised that all the children were gathered round a computer together in the dark. The oldest daughter was at the controls of a game which they were all intently involved in watching, and about which they were communicating.

Adults with autism can clearly benefit, too. In a residential home run by Autism London, a computer was recently installed for staff. Within a week, half the residents had used the new machine. The special benefits that can bring both people with autism and their carers are listed here.

### Therapeutic and educational benefits of interacting with computers

- Anyone with autism is happy to accept positive cotropical attention: computer monitors, with their precise cursor movements, greatly facilitate the would-be sharer's ability to recognise the individual's current focus of interest, ie computers make joining in really easy.
- If someone else is joining in, they and their cotropical interventions may be highly welcome.
- The autistic individual's long-term acceptance and concern for the sharer may in turn be enhanced or initiated by these interactions.
- The autistic individual may become motivated to show and share their achievements.
- The autistic individual may become motivated to speak, to the computer, or to an other.
- The autistic individual may become motivated to read.
- The autistic individual may key in to cause and effect.
- By presenting autistic individuals with outward manifestations of their thoughts, computers may potentiate reflection (Jordan and Powell, 1990; Williams, 1992)
- By giving autistic individuals power and scope, as well as potentiating reflection, it may help develop agency and self-awareness and greatly increase their self-esteem, and optimism.
- Using a computer with an autistic individual may greatly increase the sharer's respect and optimism, by revealing unobvious purposeful intelligence.

## Cotropical Engagement Facilitated

'Start where the child is' can be hard advice to follow if the child is into headbanging or walking back and forth along the cracks between floorboards or ceaselessly tapping and banging or throwing everything behind the sofa. Even when someone is willing to try to tune in to those activities or others, it is not always possible to work out exactly what does occupy the child's interest, or how to join in with it or make relevant comments which are not unwelcome. Since that is a key to any relationship, it is of high importance in establishing the especially difficult one between autistic and non-autistic people.

Just as when people are watching a sport, it is easy to see exactly what their focus of attention is, so it is at the computer. It can be easily and precisely tuned in to, and anyone who joins the fan's attention tunnel will be welcome there. Distractions, exotropic stimuli of all kinds from irrelevant words to irrelevant police sirens outside, will be unwelcome. So long as the interactor keeps all comments as relevant as possible, does not try to put own interest to the fore, then that person will be an agreeable presence. If observers can also offer a little guidance through the software – doing their best to offer only when a perceived pause occurs – then their presence will be doubly welcome. Together, they and their autistic companion will have constructively resolved a problem. It will have gone beyond social acceptance to active engagement and effective communication.

The interactor has gone 90% of the way, but just by deploying a mouse for their own satisfaction the user has created a series of expressions which have come part way to meet the attentive other. The computer provides a sort of neutral interface through which communications can occur much more easily than is normal in autism It takes no special effort from the user, indeed no communicative intention whatever is needed from them. And it takes much less communicative effort than usual for the carer to be confidently cotropical. Mike was able to hit it off with Ferenc first time because of all this. Any carer who is not intimidated by computers has the possibility that with their aid effective communication may take place between them and their autistic charge.

## Good Communication and Mutual Concern

Carers who have worked at cotropicality may be rewarded, as I have, by finding some signs of concern for their well-being emerging. Ferenc trying to give me the video because he knew I wanted it, and his retaining that concern over many weeks so as to press the next one on me straight away, strike me as being such signs (for more about Ferenc see Murray, 1995). His willingness to relinquish to Mike his CD cases (Ferenc likes clear plastic), and his willingness to give Mike attention at the computer interface, even when not immediately furthering his own aims, plus his enthusiastic assent to the question of whether he liked Mike, all suggest that he has some level of positive feeling towards Mike as a distinct individual. I believe this feeling is motivated by the delight of having one's interests furthered, which somehow fans warm feelings towards the source of the delight. Those warm feelings seem to last beyond the bounds of the happy situation.

If part of what we hope to do in relating to people with autism is create a genuinely two-sided relationship, we may need to start in this very one-sided fashion, letting the other's interests lead, at least some of the time. Awareness of your distinctive otherness, and its value, may be initiated or enhanced. With it, perhaps, some clearer sense of self may emerge in the child (see Hobson, 1993 and for more on this issue from a 'theory of mind' perspective, see Leslie and Frith, 1985).

## Motivation to Show

Awareness of the other as sharer of one's interests, awareness of the possibility that an other may wish to join one's attention tunnel, and belief that the object in question is of value – these seem to be prerequisites of the desire to show. In his teens, Ferenc has often evinced that desire to share his view or his achievement, not just with me but with familiar staff at school. But he also wanted to show what he had done to Mike, a comparative stranger, noted with apparent gratification how impressed Mike was, and held out his hand to be shaken when Mike urged him to.

And there is Sean's example as well: the first time he spontaneously got his mother and took her somewhere to show her something was to show her his achievements on the screen. It seems that a sense of personal achievement may also be part of this activity of directing the other's attention (see below).

## Motivation of Speech

Although our interactions do not involve Ferenc being actively verbal, I do talk about what's going on or what I think the possibilities might be. He gives every appearance of reaction to relevant suggestions. So long as I direct my words along the trajectory of his interest he seems to understand quite complex utterances. The same is true for his interactions at the computer with Mike. So the computer work can promote verbal awareness even if, as in this case, it does not spur the person with autism to active language use. But computers *can* do that, witness the case of Sean's little brother who had uttered no word until he called out to the computer – now he talks to anyone, and still to the machine!

## Motivation to Read

Much software has a verbal component in its use, and must promote at least awareness of verbal forms, if not any grasp of the logic of their component parts, or their meaning in other contexts. Perhaps after a while, sufficient exposure to written words, along with the potential to survey them at one's leisure and the motivation to do so, may sometimes result in the development of genuine reading. And perhaps that, combined with the easily accessible keyboard full of letters which appear perfectly formed on the screen, may contribute to motivate writing, too. I have no case study evidence to offer on this point; these suggestions are *a priori*.

## Potentiation of Reflection

Whether employing verbal or non-verbal expression, the movements of the cursor are punctuated by decisions which leave a trail on the screen. Just as this renders the agent's interests visible to an outside observer so it renders them visible to the agent. Most of us, I believe, generate self-awareness out of other-awareness and learn reflection from that duality. It creates the psychological gap necessary before an attempt can be made to look back with a perspective. Without that gap, recollection is probably mainly a matter of reviving a feeling state with no possibility of taking a view of that state, let alone controlling it or comparing it with any alternative states. Planning would go no further than the imagination could take it within the sphere of a single interest, and would presumably anticipate only the desired outcome and not any alternatives.

## Awareness of Cause and Effect

Since almost every key stroke has an effect, and that effect is predictable, the notion that those key strokes play a causal role seems utterly transparent. If there is a need to teach the concept of cause and effect, access to a computer should provide an ideal means.

## Awareness of Agency and Self

The fingers tapping the mouse buttons or keys, and feeling them yield, the eyes seeing the cursor move, and the feeling of satisfaction at all this, all co-occur over and over again. They do so in a relatively permanent medium which presents their results to the agent of their production – just as it does to any observer. Agents can observe their own agency, and can do so in their own time.

The computer is almost like a doppleganger (I owe this observation to Dr Jeff Mason, who has contributed a philosophical viewpoint to the discussions of mind, with Mike Lesser and others, which underlie the position presented here), an outward presentation of oneself – a chance to see one's self in a new sort of mirror in which time leaves a trail, and purpose is visible.

When computers also function as communication interface with another human being, then they will also help build awareness of the companionable other. A full appreciation of one's own agency must surely include awareness of a distinction between others' causal roles and one's own. Probably two-person games are among the best ways of fostering this vital aspect of self-awareness. Being socially rewarding within the peer group at school (or at home), and necessarily involving turn-taking, must underscore anyone's awareness of their own distinctness, and value as a person.

## Self-esteem, Optimism

A burgeoning, strengthening, sense of self may arise out of being an agent of successful creations. Appreciation firstly of one's own causal role and secondly of the value of its results, must go a long way towards sustaining a sense of distinctive and lasting individual potency. That must, I believe, be a crucial component of selfhood – and a vital motivator in the desire to show others one's results. The esteem of others, and their voiced appreciation – whether they are carers, siblings or peer group members – reinforces the self-esteem,

That confident power is a prerequisite of the optimistic attitude everyone needs to get through a hard world without depression. Perhaps teenage and adult autistic depression would be less commonplace if computers were more commonplace.

## Carer Optimism and Respect

Autistic behaviours can be distressing for carers, and the long-term prospects can look so bleak, despair can be inviting. Although I appreciated Ferenc's graphic skills enough to connect him with that animation program, I had no idea he would do so much so fast. Although Sean's mother felt sure of his intelligence and had faith in his potential, she had no idea he'd be able to use a mouse, let alone a keyboard. Now he's communicating more, and tapping and banging less – and his carers feel deeply encouraged by his evidently happy progress.

Seeing these normally asocial beings communicating effectively is on its own enough to promote carer optimism. Seeing their sometimes splendid creations, and realising one's own inferiority, can also be an eye-opener! As autistic behaviours go, playing with a computer must be one of the most widely acceptable. So carers will also have the pleasure of seeing their charges behaving, without any coercion, in a way which 'fits in'. And they may have the delight of having the individual with autism actually wishing to share and show their achievements.

## Next Steps

Make sure every class with an autistic child in it has at least one computer, preferably two. (Ideally every home – natural or residential – with an autistic individual should also have at least one computer.) To start with, any old computer with some graphics software will do. Use the child's achievements to argue for latest and best from your education authority – it can only be in their interests as much as the child's. Train staff or acquire volunteers who will provide the necessary support. The helpful and observant companionship I am advocating can be practised at once by anyone. But a person with some prior familiarity with the software will be much better placed to build up with the autistic person, the kind of warm mutual feelings that help the rest of us put up with each other and keep us cheerful. Accessing such feelings seems particularly hard for people with autism, and may also be particularly valuable for them. Carers should try to stay one step ahead so they can provide effective support.

Many children will find the whole experience so confidence boosting and relaxing, that their most world-excluding autistic behaviours – like Sean's tapping and banging – will occur less frequently. And, as Rutger van der Gaag of the Veldwijk Research Institute in the Netherlands puts it, the more at ease the individual is the larger their attention window, i.e. the window through which information can be taken in.

Once that comfortable relationship with computers has been established, their strictly educational potential can be accessed, individual learning programs devised, and so on (see Cenmac and NCET in Appendix). Many people with autism may go on to use modems, access the Internet, and achieve a new sort of normalisation thereby. The educational, and in particular auto didactic, possibilities are limitless. But it is their role as communication interface with people in the same space, which may prove their most valuable contribution to people who live with autism.

Entitlement to access to information technology should follow from a number of United Nations declarations notably from the Charter for Persons with Autism. The following conspicuously apply:

- The right of people with autism to live independent and full lives.
- Their right to the equipment, assistance and support services necessary to live a fully productive life with dignity and independence.
- Their right to participate and benefit from culture, entertainment, and recreation.
- Their right to equal access to and use of all facilities, services and activities in the community.
- Their right to accessible and appropriate education.

We have an obligation to provide all those to these sensitive and vulnerable people. Who knows what potential we may reveal by doing so.

## Acknowledgements

Thanks to Paul Shattock and everybody else who makes Durham a worthwhile event and genuine exchange of ideas. Thanks to Ferenc Virag for being himself, and Mike Lesser likewise. Thanks to Stuart Powell and Sarah Libby for organising me into attending their workshop; thanks to Rita Jordan, and Stuart again, for commissioning me to pursue questions about computers and autism, and Colin Nimmo likewise. Thanks to everybody at Harborough School and at my workplace, carers and cared for, for their patience and good nature. Thanks to Johan Baker for her observations on spittle, and to Helen Tworkowski for hers on empathy. And special thanks to Rosemarie Mason (of Redbridge Autistic Families Together – RAFT) for giving me so much wonderful feedback from real life in her extraordinary family, and for all the benefits her energy is bringing the world of autism. And thanks to Lesley Rahamin, Glyn Holt and Mike Blamires, for their interest, knowledge and enthusiasm.

# References

Courchesne, E. (1996) 'Abnormal cerebellar activity in autism alters cortical and subcortical systems'. Paper presented at the *Fifth Congress Autism-Europe* (Hope is not a Dream) Barcelona, May.

Dawson, G. (ed.) (1989) *Nature Diagnosis and Treatment of Autism.* London: Guilford Press.

Frith, U. (1989) *Autism: Explaining the Enigma.* Oxford: Blackwell.

Happé, F. (1994) *Autism an Introduction to Psychological Theory.* London: UCL Press.

Hobson, P. (1993) *Autism and the Development of Mind.* London: Erlbaum.

Jordan, R.R. & Powell, S.D. (1989) *The Special Curriculum Needs of Autistic Children: Learning and Thinking Skills.* London: Association of Head Teachers of Autistic Children and Adults.

Jordan, R.R. and Powell, S.D. (1995)*Understanding and Teaching Children with Autism.* Chichester: Wiley.

Leslie, A.M. & Frith, U. (1987) 'Metarepresentation and autism: how not to lose one's marbles'. *Cognition*, 27, 291–294.

Murray, D.K.C. (1995) 'An autistic friendship', in *Proceedings of the International Conference – Psychological Perspectives in Autism*, Durham University, published by the Autism Research Unit, University of Sunderland.

Sperber, D. & Wilson, D. (1986) *Relevance, Communication and Cognitition.* Oxford: Blackwell.

# Appendix

Leslie Rahamin CENMAC (Centre for MicroAssisted Communication) Eltham Green Complex, 1A Middle Park Avenue, Eltham SE9 5HL

Glyn Holt (Learning Disabilities) NCET (National Council for Educational Technology) Milburn Hill Road, Science Park, Coventry CV4 7JJ

Jim Wobus' Website for autism contacts generally: http://web.syr.edu/

# COMMENTARY

# Education as Therapy

In the opening paragraph, the author makes the point that education for children with autism necessarily involves an element of therapy and further that a computer-based learning environment is well suited to such an endeavour. We have argued this point elsewhere (Powell and Jordan, 1996) and perhaps it is worth examining evidence and exploring any implications here in the light of Murray's descriptions of learning in a computer environment.

There is a sense in which attempts at educating any child have to take account of that child's learning style and abilities (along with a number of other social and emotional factors). This truism takes on a particular significance in autism because of the fundamental way in which the thinking and learning of the individual with autism differs from that of the non-autistic in that, essentially, non-autistic learning *is* a social activity. There is a natural tension, then, between teaching, which is typically conceived of as a cultural activity involving the social construction of meaning, and autistic learning, which is necessarily of an asocial kind. In the sense that meaning is socially constructed then the world remains meaningless for the individual for whom social construction remains opaque. Of course there is meaning for the individual with autism but it is one which is derived from idiosyncratic origins and which remains personal and disconnected from the social world.

What Murray describes in her chapter is a learning environment which can be to an extent determined by the learner. It is an environment which is not necessarily socially mediated. How can this environment be described as therapeutic? The way in which Murray describes the advantages of the computer environment and later her own interactions with Ferenc in part answers this question. The computer is not an immediate part of any social scenario. Certainly, it can become one and indeed it can be designed to be one. But, it starts out as a thing to act upon and one which responds in a predictable way. Two people acting upon this thing then are not necessarily engaged with each other. The therapy, if there is any, is in the way in which the computer (or more properly the computer program) exists as an entity which enables two people to engage with each other because they are in fact engaging with this third party, this inanimate, asocial, reflecting response mechanism. In short, Murray and Ferenc learn to interact with each other through action upon this mechanism.

The dimension which may justify the label of *therapy* is that both Murray and Ferenc are enabled to learn. Just as the therapist and client are engaged in a joint enterprise to understand (i.e. to understand the client and the way in which he/she is able to relate to the world) so are the two protagonists in this chapter. It is clear from the way in which Murray writes as well as the content of her chapter that she has experienced the computer as a medium in which she has been enabled to learn about Ferenc and his way of seeing and understanding the world. And this kind of learning has been reciprocated by Ferenc himself who has learned something of Murray.

Of course, computers could be used to train the child with autism to perform certain tasks. But that is not what occurs in the case of Ferenc. The point of all this for the teacher is that the computer offers choice and the potential to synthesise education and therapy. Precisely because of its asocial possibilities it becomes an ideal vehicle for learning together and learning about each other. This is not to deny its usefulness as a way of training. Training is often an essential precursor to education and as such needs to be valued. What Murray offers in her chapter is a notion of using computers which goes beyond the apparent useful functions of training in particular skills and knowledge and enters an altogether richer domain.

## Using the Child's Interests

Just as we saw above, that there can be a paradox in an asocial medium being used ultimately for social learning, there is a paradox in teaching individuals with autism in that only when we truly enter their focus of interest, can they begin to enter ours. The author offers a convincing argument for why this is so and a moving account of how it was achieved with Ferenc through the use of computers. The author also deals with the worries voiced by many teachers and carers, with respect to the use of computers with people with autism, that the individual will become increasingly obsessive and less interested in people. In doing so, she raises another paradox, that engaging with the child in an obsessive interest can make it less obsessive (in that it can make the child more open to 'advice' and modification of otherwise obsessive routines) and that an asocial medium can be used to mediate a social relationship. The particular reasons for the attraction of computers for people with autism are expressed eloquently in the chapter, as are the particular benefits of using computers as the joint focus of attention in teaching.

## Reference

Powell, S.D. and Jordan, R.R. (1996) 'Education, therapy and autism: a special case?' in *Proceedings of the International Conference – 'Therapeutic Intervention in Autism: Perspectives from Research and Practice.* Durham University, published by the Autism Research Unit, University of Sunderland.

# CHAPTER 8

# Assessment

Staff at the Helen Allison School (NAS)  Compiled by Malcolm.W.Taylor
With special thanks for their contributions to
Mary Lewis, Linda Hall, Joanne Neill, Joan Ratcliffe, Shaun Thorogood
With acknowledgements to
Jacqui Ashton Smith, Mike Collins, Joanne Douglas

## Introduction

The following chapter reflects upon a range of issues concerning assessment that have been highlighted by staff working with children with autism at the Helen Allison School (National Autistic Society – NAS). It has been well documented (e.g. Jordan and Powell, 1995) that there are difficulties in the area of assessment for pupils with autism. We have attempted to show here how an awareness of these general difficulties has informed our practice at the school and we have illustrated specific issues from our own observations. A central theme of this is the way in which children are encouraged to reflect on their own performance and develop their own self-assessment skills.

One of the most important aspects that comes out of this work is the fact that assessment needs to be seen as part of an ongoing process of developing an awareness of the child's strengths and needs. The systems set up within the school encourage all involved in the child's welfare to be continually re-evaluating observations concerning a child's abilities or performances and these input directly to the support procedures offered to that child. Thus formal and informal assessment procedures are seen as part of the everyday work with the children. It is necessary for all those supporting the child to have adequate opportunities to discuss their observations. This allows the generation and analysis of theories concerning the child's skills, support procedures and areas of difficulty to take place. It is clear that the way in which the children perceive their own skill development and how they learn to reflect on their achievements (so as to build connections between different areas of their lives) is also an essential aspect of this overall process.

The complex nature of the difficulties experienced by persons with autism are such that there is a need for wide-ranging assessment over a broad area of skills and needs. The most obvious point concerning assessment of skills is the need for assessment of skill performance in a range of settings and different contexts. It is very clear that children with autism learn to carry out certain skills in specific contexts but when presented with what may seem to an outside observer as a very similar context, are seemingly unable to carry out the task. This necessitates the need for generalisation training to be built into any programme of teaching. At the same time it is important to assess where possible what specific features of the environment are important for the child, in order to allow them to carry out the skill.

## Assessment Procedures Used in the School

There are a range of assessment procedures in the school in question which contribute to teachers' overall knowledge about the child. The school offers a broad curriculum including all areas of the National Curriculum differentiated to meet the individual needs of the child. The school curriculum has a specific focus on personal and social skills, communication skills, skills for independent living, self-care skills, leisure skills and integration activities. The personal and social education programmes for each child make specific reference to observed impairments in social interaction, social communication, social imagination and the narrowness or repetitive pattern of their activities. Thus it is necessary to have a clear assessment of these areas. This is carried out through a process of informal and formal sessions of observation, discussion with parents, other involved individuals outside the school, school based staff and residential staff. Equally important are the personal reflections from the children themselves. Through this process of self-reflection and the structuring of activities within the school to support this, it is hoped that the children will develop some of the broader thinking skills and an increased awareness of their own ability to solve problems.

Within the school the ongoing assessment of the child is carried out through the system of termly Individual Education Plans (IEP) covering work in all areas including the 24 hour curriculum activities. These are written up by class based and residential staff in conjunction with parents who discuss the plan formally on a termly basis as well as during regular informal discussions. The targets on the IEP therefore form the basis of assessment of progress across all areas of the curriculum. The targets on the individual education plan are further broken down into curriculum recording sheets to monitor progress in each school based area and 24 hour curriculum planning sheets which monitor progress towards the targets set for residential activities.

Prior to the child's annual review, a report of the child's progress is written by staff at the school who are directly involved with the child. This is then sent to parents for additional comments as well as feedback from the child. These forms written by, or with comments dictated by the child, have proved to be a valuable source of information for assessment. This allows the pupil to have time to think over issues and put them forward away from the pressures of the formal review. At the annual review meeting, attended by parents, the child and representatives of outside bodies, the *Statement of Educational Needs* is reviewed to discuss any proposed amendments necessary which are then sent on to the child's Local Authority for consideration. This is therefore a further opportunity for pupils to review their own development and progress. These systems allow a clear connection to be made between the formal statement of educational need, the annual review report and the individual education plan. Thus the process of assessment can be seen to directly affect programmes put in place to meet the needs of the child.

## Core Curriculum Areas

In each subject area the child's skills are assessed using individual record sheets showing the attainment of specific behaviours or skills in that area. These tick boxes for each target are marked with the following scheme. There are four columns marked beside each target where the teacher records the progress made by dating the appropriate column box. There is additional space for comments to be made. The four columns show a progressive increase in competence from needing a high level of prompt to carrying out the skill consistently without support. These individual curriculum sheets provide the basis for assessment in each subject area.

However, as well as this type of recording, a great deal of informal information is gathered from day to day observations which give insight to how the child is understanding or thinking about various tasks. This information is recorded by staff in the form of diary records either as part of the school classroom records or in the home/residential/school books. In this way all those involved with the child are made aware of the issues. These can then be discussed further and their relevance for planning activities reflected upon.

### Mathematics

The subject of mathematics, generally involving as it does right or wrong answers, gives the opportunity for pupils to take some control over the assessment of their progress using answer books. We have found this to be of particular use both in the development of self awareness and independence and also in raising pupils' general level of self confidence. One particular child had a great deal of difficulty accepting any form of correction despite attempts to put this in a positive manner. The process of initially checking the answers himself has helped him to be in control of this process and then accept guidance from others without becoming upset. Allied to this is the issue that many children with autism find the idea of work being changed by correction difficult, and they want their initial version to be the correct one. Both of these responses can be interpreted in terms of difficulties with flexibility of thought as it is the process of changing their initial answer that is difficult as well as accepting that their answer, once written, is not the correct one.

The generalisation issues described earlier in this chapter are particularly important when working on practical tasks in mathematics. To this end, when working on the use of money, it is important to use real money and assess the child's understanding of its use in a range of settings. To do this, money skills are taught in a range of ways both in classroom activities linked to work cards and in school based and community based situations. This is one area where the need for a full community based programme of education is essential. Skills need to be taught and assessed in settings where they are going to be used. Once a concept, such as the identification and use of certain coins, has been taught and understood it is important that the child's use of the skill is assessed with other individuals such as the child's parents. The teaching of these skills, if for example using a gradual fading of prompts, has to be carefully monitored at each stage to ensure that those supporting the child are consistent in their use of prompts. For instance, it has been observed that, despite difficulties with social gaze and joint attention, some individuals are able to use the direction of the visual gaze of others to cue their response. Those working with children therefore have to continually be aware of the prompts they may be giving, such as looking at the right coin, when assessing performance.

There are many problem solving tasks in mathematics that encourage children to reflect on their own thinking and understanding of the task being carried out. One of the most difficult areas of mathematical ability for children with autism is the estimation of measurements. We have found that some children who may be able to carry out complex mathematical operations can still have a great deal of difficulty estimating the costs of day to day purchases. This can be worked on by carrying out surveys of items in local shops. Producing a graph of these figures helps give a visual reference to reinforce the difference between, for instance, the cost of a car and everyday shopping items.

The use of mathematics schemes can be useful in the classroom though it has to be remembered that pupils with autism are likely to require far more detailed assessment than the accompanying schedules or records of progress used in these. As in other subjects, at Helen Allison we use a comprehensive checklist of mathematical objectives to assess progress. This also offers suggestions for future activities and identifies any areas at an early stage that the child appears not yet to have grasped.

## English

The assessment of reading skills involves looking at the ability of the child both to decode the text and show some understanding of the words he/she has 'read'. The type of reading material being used must also be taken into account when assessing reading. Many children with autism will happily read books of factual information yet may find story books involving elements of fantasy both difficult and boring.

Hyperlexia, where children are able to read text beyond their level of understanding, is again well documented in pupils with autism. It is important therefore for there to be an increased focus on comprehension exercises to assess reading performance. When using the *Neale Analysis of Reading Ability* (Neale, 1988) in the school it is clear that many children who can read the text accurately have difficulty with the comprehension questions. Even if the child has understood the passage well, many of the comprehension questions involving thinking at a metacognitive level, such as those concerning motivations for certain behaviours or the possible thoughts/emotions of characters in the story, will inevitably prove difficult for children with autism. Therefore, it is necessary when assessing reading to have a clear idea of the type of information required by the child to answer such questions. If the purpose of the assessment is to look at the child's understanding of the text, then questions concerning the factual content are of more use. When working in this area we have found it useful to devise assessments and comprehension exercises using factual books that the children enjoy.

The assessment of comprehension can be broken down further by using graded levels of prompts in the instructions. One example of this is the use of a word or phrase in the question that is the same as that used in the text. One child when working on this, was not able to answer a question 'What is the name of the . . .?'. Yet the child was able to answer when the question was rephrased 'What was the . . . called?'. This was due to the fact that the word 'called' was in the text and therefore functioned as a cue to the answer. The outcome of this type of assessment can also help differentiate the level of understanding depending on whether the child copies the sentence in the text or rephrases it in some way for their answer.

The contextual elements in the development of reading skills, or preparedness of children to read, must again clearly be taken into account when assessing skill development. There have been several children at the school who developed reading skills but were only prepared to use or demonstrate them in certain contexts. Those children with good visual memories may be able to remember small elements about flashcards when working on key words and therefore need to be exposed to a range of presentations of the word to avoid over reliance on these cues. The assessment of their knowledge of these words needs to take into account the style of presentation.

When working on spelling it has been found useful to get children to identify words in their own work that they are unsure of, and then check them using a dictionary. This is clearly difficult, although it does give a first stage of self-reflection to this process. One of the most common errors is the failure to use contextual information to choose between two identical sounding but differently spelt words. One older pupil in the school developed a long list of these with an explanation of the different contexts. He was then able to check these each time he used them and when taking time to think each one out was eventually able to spell them correctly.

The understanding of the context or audience for a particular piece of writing proves an area of difficulty for many children who have literacy skills at this level. Some children may learn to use phrases which makes their writing sound interesting. However these may look out of place in a piece of writing if often repeated or used in an inappropriate manner. The application of some of this language and difficulties in understanding different styles of writing, clearly reflects the social difficulties of children with autism. To help develop self-awareness of these issues, a range of strategies can be used. With some of the older pupils this has been worked on by staff reading out the phrases used in a way that emphasises their inappropriateness. Staff then read out a more appropriate piece of writing for the set context and discuss the difference. Through discussion of when people are most likely to use certain phrases (based on known events where possible) and by staff acting out possible responses to the language used, it has been possible to develop some understanding of these issues. It must be acknowledged, however, that, despite developing rules for when to use certain phrases, the generalisation of these skills through self reflection and self appraisal has proved to be particularly difficult for students in our experience.

### Science

The practical nature of science work in the school clearly lends itself to assessment of the factual elements covered in the lesson, through discussion or writing, as well as the development of reflective skills. A discussion of the practical activity at the beginning of the session makes it possible to elicit suggestions of what might happen in this particular exercise and from this draw up lists of observations to be made. These can then be phrased in simple questions requiring precise observation. In this way the child can go from a very open task of observing a series of events to a more focused study with a clear visual structure.

This work links clearly with the National Curriculum programme of study concerning experimental and investigative science. The assessment of pupils progress in this area is partly carried out by recording of statements made in discussions concerning the process of investigation, as well as evidence concerning the detail of the child's observations and the strategies used to make these. This work can range from the way in which a child at an early level investigates objects, such as testing their properties through direct manipulation, to the complexity of experimental procedures suggested by another.

An important aspect of developing the ability to reflect on one's thinking and form theoretical models, is the level of self-confidence of the child and lack of fear of getting things wrong. To aid this process, ideas from pupils are carefully supported and encouraged with adults describing how ideas can change over time as knowledge develops. Giving personal examples of mistakes we as a member of staff have made on a day to day basis can further help children learn the concept of accepting being wrong.

## Other Curriculum Areas

The process of self-assessment can be seen in a range of other curriculum areas in the school. In art/craft activities, for instance, the planning of the work involves decisions about the types of materials to be used and the sequence of events to be followed. As the piece of work develops, decisions need to be made as to what steps are to be taken next. This process encourages children to reflect on their actions by associating them with the effect on the product. These activities also allow for a range of problem solving questions to be asked. This is shown for example in the work of one young child who enjoys making dinosaurs. He had to decide how long a tail he could make without it snapping off and then where to place the finished article so it was safe.

In early play activities there are opportunities for discussing play equipment with the children in terms of how many people can play with an object, deciding who is going to use what and what it could be used for. These types of question encourage simple choices to be made which are a precursor to more complex problem solving and self-reflection skills. Informal recording of the statements made by children at these times forms a basis for further discussion with parents and other staff so as to plan future activities.

## Social Communication and Interaction skills

The following examples show how certain approaches can help develop a greater awareness of self through structured reflection on day to day events. The work on assessing the importance of news events to others may help in developing retrieval systems or future encoding of events using an emotional/importance link as described by Jordan and Powell (1995).

To encourage reflection in group discussion, children are encouraged not only to discuss events that have taken place at home or at school but also to attempt to make judgements about what are generally seen as important events. In one class children have worked on thinking this through, using a set of questions. Examples of these are 'Does the event take place every week?' so as to reflect on its importance or interest to others. By using these set criteria to evaluate what may be interesting to others, this group of children have shown significant development in the interest level of their language. This development can be assessed in terms of the level of prompts necessary to self question the importance of the event. One aspect of this has been the realisation that they do not have to say anything if they feel there is no significant piece of news to relate.

Another important skill in these sessions was an exercise in choosing three important things that have happened and describing them in the order of perceived importance rather than the order in which they took place. This was to encourage a young man to think about the interest shown by others in his news and get out of the habit of describing things in a monotonous diary like form. Getting feedback from the group and voting on the most interesting news item has also helped in this process.

At a simpler level, getting pupils to say what others have told them in discussions or to ask questions of others helps, in the development of awareness of others and consequent social interaction. The use of photographs so that individuals can recognise and point to others is also of use for those at an early stage of development of these skills. Photographs are often used generally in group discussions as they allow for simple descriptive information as well as being a catalyst for more open questions to be placed to the group. This also provides a visual link between the life of the pupil at home to that of school so as to build an awareness of a more integrated view of life by the pupil. One interesting extension of this was the use of a Dictaphone with a pupil living in a separate residential unit but attending the school. The pupil enjoyed school based staff recording events on the tape describing his work at school and also the residential staff informing the school of his activities there. This gave the pupil an opportunity to reflect on his activities in both settings in a direct way as he heard the voices of the people involved and other sounds associated with the locations and events.

This work leads onto the use of video in the development of self-assessment as well as in formal assessment. Children in the school are regularly recorded on video for a range of assessment purposes. An informal viewing and qualitative analysis of this information will often lead to general observations about children's behaviour that can be easily missed when working in the classroom. For example, the videoing of play behaviour of the young children will often pick up the very short examples of social interaction such as an exchange of toys and eye contact or joint sharing of an activity. This information is of particular use when discussing play behaviour, relationships with siblings and strategies to further encourage this, with parents. It is also very useful to have, as a long-term record of the behaviour of the child, to show development over an extended period of time. Many of the children at the school enjoy looking at film of themselves and others at an earlier age and this can also lead onto discussions about growth and change.

The use of video film as part of a record of achievement has been beneficial to many pupils who have enjoyed showing examples of their achievements in a range of areas to others. Again this medium is particularly useful in encouraging pupils to make observations about their task performance on the activity which forms part of their self-assessment.

With a group of pupils in the Key stage 4 transition class of the school, video has been used in a specific manner to develop self reflection of their social skills. This group attends a weekly integration social group at the local mainstream comprehensive school. While there, the pupils take part in a range of social activities such as playing pool, listening to music and playing table top games. The pupils have taken a video of this activity on a number of occasions and viewed it on returning to school. The pupils have been encouraged to look at how often they are talking to or generally interacting with others. It has been interesting to note that some pupils have observed themselves not interacting and been surprised by this. One pupil saw himself walk away from a game of pool in the middle of the game to study something in the room. He observed that he didn't remember doing this and commented on the actions of the other pupil playing pool. This self-assessment of their social behaviour allowed the pupils in the group to set themselves informal objectives concerning social behaviour for future sessions. This type of self-assessment needs to be sensitively presented, to avoid producing anxiety or feelings of failure in youngsters with autism, but it is clear from this example and other work with older students, that pupils can benefit significantly from this type of self-assessment. It has been shown that these observations allow the pupils to become aware of their behaviour and make predictions about how others may perceive their social behaviour. This in turn has led to work on developing more appropriate social behaviour.

**Social behaviour**

One approach to the development of social behaviour that has proved to be most successful has been the use of class discussions centred around a topic. These have been structured in one class by using a series of books on issues such as interrupting, tantrums etc. (Berry, 1984). In these sessions the whole class read and discuss each page of the book which presents the issue in a simple cartoon form. When discussing tantrums, one pupil, who had been having tantrums at home, started to look away from the group and, when asked about them, she described the tantrums at home. She said in the discussions 'It's not good to have tantrums, mummy not happy'. She then took the book home that evening and read it with her mother. After reading it at home she said 'no more tantrums' she then broke a plate and has not had a tantrum at home to date. This appears to be an example of where a classroom activity brought out an issue from home and the process of self-reflection or possibly the fact she knew others at school knew of the behaviour lead to a significant change.

There have been situations where the use of a checklist of specific social behaviours has led to a reduction in anti-social behaviour. The checklist seems to serve as a visual reminder which prompts its reduction. An example of this is the use of a ticklist for a pupil to fill in to show he had refrained from swearing . Other examples are visual lists of rules, or prompts to carry out behaviours incompatible with the challenging behaviour. The use of rules written out by pupils in conjunction with members of staff has been shown to be particularly effective in developing more appropriate social behaviour for many pupils. There are clearly several areas to this. The fact that the pupil has been involved in drafting the rules gives a sense of involvement and individual responsibility. The fact that the pupil is involved in choosing their own reinforcers for appropriate behaviour is also more likely to make them more effective. The act of writing these rules down helps clarify exactly what is required in terms of observable behaviour or concrete actions of the child.

It has been clear, using these systems of self-assessment of behaviour, how difficult it is for some intellectually able children to remember or concentrate on exactly what it is they have to do. By having a visual list of guidance they can be directed to this to check their behaviour, to remove the interpersonal conflict of being told what to do by a member of staff. There are several children in the school who appear to find it easier to do something because it says so on a list, rather than because they have been asked to by someone.

The assessment of challenging behaviour exhibited by any pupil in the school is based on a full functional analysis of the behaviour described as the STAR approach in work by Zarkowska and Clements (1994). This assessment involves all those involved with the pupil so that a comprehensive picture of the setting conditions, specific triggers, actions and results connected with this behaviour can be built up. This assessment of the behaviour then leads to programmes to develop the pupils' self-management skills and a reduction in the challenging behaviour.

It is interesting to note that, with the ability to carry out self-assessment, some pupils have been able to become aware of some of the issues related to their challenging behaviour. One older pupil who exhibits a high level of physically challenging behaviour recently announced that he was not going to watch certain of his videos anymore as he said they made him excited and violent. It had been observed by those working with this pupil that his obsessional fixation on violence would often lead to incidents of challenging behaviour and this had been discussed with him on a range of occasions before. This particular pupil when calm will also talk about not wanting to be violent and how he does not want to upset others. These behaviours clearly show that some pupils with autism have the ability to reflect on their behaviours and carry out actions to enable some change in their patterns of behaviour.

## Emotional development

There has been some interesting work carried out in the school looking at pupils' ability to further their awareness and understanding of emotional states. Using simple worksheets, pupils have described situations in which they have experienced feelings such as loneliness, worry, nervousness, happiness, etc. As well as describing these situations they have reflected on the physical states that accompanied these feelings. This is intended to help develop an awareness of these physical reactions so as to help pupils recognise their reactions to situations and reflect on their own emotional states. Discussing these emotional states and the pupils' examples, such as feeling nervous when meeting new people, or being interviewed, has led on to discussions and role play in how to cope with these feelings. Examples of this would be role play concerning making a complaint in a shop and how to cope with people not listening to you or with others becoming angry.

At the same time as working on this, one group of older students have also been working on self-advocacy skills by running their own students' group. Points from this then go forward to staff meetings to input on decisions effecting activities or the general organisation of the Post-16 Unit. It has been interesting to note the abilities of some pupils to persuade others to take part in the group. There has been a significant growth in the self-confidence shown by these pupils through this empowerment process which has allowed them to self assess there own activities and opportunities as well as their personal development.

Other work on self-awareness has involved pupils stating what they feel they are good at and what they feel they need help with. Extensions of these are asking who they admire or would like to be like and why. An excellent resource, for some of the types of language exercise described, is the Social Use of Language Programme (Rinaldi, 1992) which contains clear assessment records.

## Record of Achievement/Transition Planning

The use of the National Record of Achievement in schools has given an increased emphasis to the pupils' self assessment of skills, abilities and progress. For pupils with autism this presents a significant challenge to reflect on their own achievements and general personal qualities. The Record of Achievement process involves pupils looking at all areas of their lives both within and outside school to put forward a positive picture of their personal qualities and to show evidence of personal involvement in future planning.

The formal Record of Achievement consists of a folder containing a series of statements concerning the individual. The statements concerning school achievements and experiences, the personal statement and the individual action plan all involve significant self-assessment skills for the pupil. Accompanying the record of achievement the pupils have a range of supporting evidence such as video, photographs and examples of work.

The pupils have worked on developing their Record of Achievement by reviewing practical examples of their work across the curriculum. They have attempted to state what they felt they had learned and achieved in each area. This has been carried out in a range of ways.

The day to day work with the pupils involves a continual process of discussing what they are working on, what they did in their last session, and how they relate together. Pupils will regularly write down, or have written for them, details of what they have done in each session. This can be in the form of notes on comments they have made or may be in the form of check lists such as task analysis sheets. For some pupils the use of task analysis sheets helps structure their work objectives and these can be presented in a pictorial form if necessary for the pupil to tick. When looking back over an activity at the end of a course, the pupils then have a record of what they heave been working on and can discuss the amount of assistance they required to achieve their objectives and how they have progressed. Here again the use of video has been useful. One example is the review of skills in a work experience setting. One group of pupils watching themselves cleaning a local cafe/bar led to various observations as to who was doing what. These straightforward observations can then be developed into broader statements of self assessment with the pupil.

The individual action planning with the students has involved support from the local careers service helping plan access to leisure, training, residential support and work opportunities for the pupils. This not only helps reinforce the individual's role in the assessment of future needs, but puts this process forward so it is seen by the pupil as involving mainstream services used by all members of the community. The type of action planning that takes place from the child's fourteenth birthday with the drawing up of a transition plan in line with the Code of Practice (DFE 1994) is another important feature of this process. This places a statutory duty to involve pupils in contributing to the transition plan and making positive decisions about their future. In order to do this, pupils with autism clearly need to be working on developing these self-assessment and evaluation skills over their whole school career.

The personal statements can pull together information from a range of activities such as language work on things the individual likes and additionally through a series of discussions on different areas. Pupils, when working on this type of activity regularly in a supportive environment, have shown a developing willingness to not only make statements about specific activities but also to begin to draw this together into more general statements about their personal qualities. Clearly this type of work cannot be carried out in isolation in a few set sessions, but needs to come about as a result of an overall supportive and reflective culture being present in the organisation the student is placed in. The pupils do require time to work with individual members of staff who know them well, to pull together this information into their final statements.

One of the most successful examples we have of this was the recent leaving assembly for some of the pupils at the end of their time at school. Two pupils were able to come up on the stage and talk at length about their life at the school over several years. This included incidents they remembered, examples of how they had changed and what they felt they had learnt over their time at school. One pupil talked at length about how he remembered not talking to anyone at all when he first came to school. He then described how a tape recorder was used to encourage him and how he then became prepared to speak at school. He also told the audience how he felt he had become more self-confident over time and was now able to travel on his own and attend his college course. This is clearly the end product of a great deal of work that the pupils have carried out over several years. It shows that, with the appropriate opportunities, pupils with autism can develop the ability to develop a certain level of self-awareness and reflect on their progress in a range of areas over time.

## References

Berry, J. (1984) *Let's Talk About Interrupting.* Danbury: Grolier Enterprises Corp.

Department For Education (1994) *Code of Practice on the Identification and Assessment of Special Educational Needs.* London: DFE Publications.

Jordan, R.R. & Powell, S.D. (1995) *Understanding and Teaching Children with Autism.* Chichester: Wiley.

Neale, M. (1988) *Neale Analysis of Reading Ability.* Windsor: NFER-Nelson.

Rinaldi, W. (1992) *The Social Use of Language Programme.* Windsor: NFER-Nelson.

Zarkowska, E. & Clements, J. (1994) *Problem Behaviour and People with Severe Learning Difficulties, The STAR Approach.* London: Chapman and Hall.

## COMMENTARY

## Purpose of Assessment

An important point is made about the need to look to the purpose of assessment. For example, if the purpose is to look at the child's literal understanding of text, then questions concerning factual content are the most likely to produce a fair assessment, but this will say nothing about the ability to understand narrative forms. It is not a matter of simply choosing an area within which the child with autism is able to function relatively well. Rather it is a matter of maintaining a focus on what information is required from the assessment. This principle is, of course, applicable to all kinds of assessment but in autism this principle takes on a unique dimension because the areas and levels of difficulty in autism are often sharply differentiated and idiosyncratic.

## Specific Cueing

The points that we made in Chapter 1, concerning the way in which specific cues operate in autistic memory, is well illustrated in this chapter where the child fails to answer the question until it is rephrased containing the original form of words. This example emphasises the sensitivity to the autistic way of thinking that is required in teaching in autism and also illustrates an issue related to the purpose of assessment. If assessment is merely normative (as in national testing), then it is appropriate to use standardised ways of assessing. But this kind of assessment is seldom of much use to the teacher and cannot serve as the kind of diagnostic assessment needed to attempt to understand the processes of the child's learning, as well as the products. For the latter exercise, all kinds of specific cueing may be needed, in an effort to obtain the child's optimum performance. This will not only give information on what the child can demonstrate when the conditions are right (and, crucially, when he or she understands what is required), but also on the strategies that are most useful for that child in reaching that attainment. It also illustrates the constraints on learning and the limits to understanding that depends on such specific cueing. In that way, it is not just the results of assessment that inform practice, but the way that assessment is carried out.

## Use of Video

The use of video as a way of enabling individuals with autism to self-assess their social behaviours is interesting, in as much as it shows how 'unaware' they can be about social situations. But the authors are right to point to the fact that this 'unawareness' is not total and that the process of assessment (the use of video) can be part of the learning process itself. Of course, as the authors also point out, the more aware the students become, the more danger there is in terms of increasing a sense of failure, as they witness their 'mistakes'. Self-assessment will always carry this danger as part of its success, as we point out below. Video assessment, of course, is not just useful in self-assessment but in capturing the way in which tasks are tackled and the timing of these, in ways that are difficult to capture through checklist assessment. A video can be more than a 'record' of achievement or failure; it shows the process and gives the teacher another chance to 'step outside' of a situation and observe what is going on. Watching a video of one's own teaching can be the most useful (if salutary) experience as we begin to see the points where we intervened too quickly, so the child did not get a chance to respond, or where our words or instructions were confusing. It can also be revelatory in showing us what the visual and the aural environments are really like in 'objective' terms, freed from the influence of our own selective attention to what our intentions are. It is only then that we hear how many distracting noises there really are in the classroom or we see the child's difficulties in attending visually to the task when it is surrounded by visual clutter that we have somehow 'ignored' in the actual situation. If the world appears as a kind of video to people with autism (because the selective attention that comes from our own purposes just does not happen) then viewing a video of it, may give us an insight into 'their' world.

## Self-Assessment

But we also want to use this example to highlight the issue about teachers' perception of changing characteristics in their students and the ways in which these are assessed. It is true that many individuals with autism do not suffer from social embarrassment, since this requires awareness of how our behaviour appears to others and the cultural norms for that kind of behaviour. Yet, as we hope this book illustrates, the difficulties by which autism is defined are just that – difficulties, not complete deficits. Development over the years and good teaching will affect those difficulties and (at least in the more able) lead to more awareness of how behaviour is seen by others. As teachers, we must remember that, although the person may retain their autism (in our view, their particular style of thinking and learning) through their education, that does not mean that they will retain their behaviours or even their particular difficulties. It is always surprising to find schools that have assiduously taught children (to use the example here) about how others think and feel and about the social norms related to their own behaviour, and yet do not take account of the changes that might have arisen as a result of this teaching, when it comes to assessment. In other words, assessment itself needs to be a reflective process. In using video as a form of self-assessment of the performance of certain skills, we can also assess the pupils' responses to the video as evidence of their increasing awareness of the very things we have been trying to teach. Good curriculum practice for pupils with autism will have personal and social education at the heart of it, as we pointed out in Chapter 2, and assessment must also recognise this, and not leave it (as it is in the education of the non-autistic) as a mere unassessed by-product . In a recursive way, the ability to profit from self-assessment, also needs to be assessed.

# CHAPTER 9

# Communication

Gina Davies

## Introduction

This chapter describes the approach that is used in the 'Little Group', a special needs nursery for children with complex communication problems, where speech and language therapy is fully integrated into all aspects of work with the children. While this work is currently targeting the pre-school child and the child in the early years of school placement, it is suggested that it has relevance to developing functional communication skills far beyond this age group.

One of the most striking aspects of communicating with children within the autistic spectrum is that it feels difficult or awkward. It is important to recognise that for those of us without special needs, communication is an attractive goal in itself, and that the motivation for us to communicate is powerful. Adults who are themselves competent communicators and who may be experienced with children often feel puzzled after talking to children with autism and yet they find it hard to say exactly why this is so. It is recognition of this difficulty in bringing into play the elements of interaction which are fundamental to communication that is, in my view, critical to making speech and language therapy intervention effective.

## Speech and Communication in Autism

The lack of speech is often the first symptom that is overtly recognised by both parents and professionals as marking a child out as needing help. A referral to a speech and language therapist usually follows, and parents may then hope that this will solve all the problems that arise. It is all too easy to follow the parents anxiety 'if only he would talk . . .' and to become overly focused on words. However, it is important to stress at the outset that the lack of speech is only a symptom of a more fundamental problem that needs to be openly discussed with all those involved if intervention is to address the child's problems appropriately (Jordan, 1993). Everyone needs to accept that the principles of communication should be developed before words are understood or uttered. These principles must be a priority of intervention and continue to be a priority when words do emerge.

From my experience, I suggest that knowledge of normal developmental patterns can give therapeutic intervention greater sensitivity. Traditional approaches may fail to take into account the impact the child has on those around them, most noticeably the way that parents' communication is disturbed or disrupted (Brooks-Gunn and Lewis, 1984; Murray and Trevarthen, 1986; Wasserman et al., 1988). It is also necessary to acknowledge that if the child disturbs the parents' communication then such disturbance is also likely occur in the communication of all those working with the child (Smith and Leinonen, 1992). This, then, might further limit the child's opportunities to learn communication and thus a negative spiral is begun. The aim underlying the approach described in this chapter is to use knowledge of normal development of communication to construct a progression in therapeutic intervention, and to limit the disturbance to interaction patterns, that result from the child's difficulties.

## The Development of Communication

Two way interaction between child and adult starts very early; it is observable two hours after birth (Clarkson and Berg, 1983). This very early interaction is already two way communication in which both newborn baby and adult take an active role. Very young babies show an interest in faces: they will seek them out and look at them carefully (Kaye, 1982). They also show a preference for animated over still or neutral faces. There is a developmental sequence to the emergence of eye contact skills, with eye contact being used to engage with adults, to signal 'more', and to direct the adult's attention (Butterworth, 1991; Crnic et al., 1983). Babies are sensitive to, and respond to, adults' patterns of eye contact. They focus their attention on the speaker through a combination of eye contact, whole body alertness and movements (Kaye, 1982).

They also fill their turn in the interaction process by using these signals to actively respond. This responsiveness, later including vocalisations and words, becomes an increasingly sophisticated two way process of communication (Stern, 1974). Babies learn quickly how to use crying to alert the adults to distress or demands; they progress to using vocalisations to take turns in interaction and sounds to attract attention and trigger adults into interaction (Bruner, 1975). At six to eight weeks (typically) babies develop the ability to smile and they use this powerful social mechanism with increasing skill, both to initiate and to prolong interaction. Also, they demonstrate the ability to imitate very early, copying open mouth postures and facial movements (Trevarthen et al., 1996). These skills quickly become incorporated into interaction: mothers often copy expressions or mouth postures that the child makes and make comments or interpretations of their meaning. Indeed imitation often forms the basis of a simple game that involves turn taking, with the parent actively attributing meaning and purpose to the child's actions (Bruner, 1975; Kaye, 1979). Again, babies use eye pointing, hand reaching and later finger pointing as a means of stimulating the adult to name objects or events around them.

Mothers tend to modify their speech to a greater extent when the child is present (Cross, 1977; Snow, 1972;1977). The younger the child the greater the number of modifications made by adults (who tend to judge age on the basis of size). Interestingly, childless adults make the same number of modifications, even if to a slightly lesser degree (Snow, 1986), which emphasises the innate quality of these skills. Mothers simplify their speech, using feedback received from the child to guide their language levels. Sentence length is reduced which simplifies grammatical structures. Higher pitches and exaggerated intonation patterns help fix the child's attention and repetition is used, thus increasing the child's chance of processing language. Mothers typically talk to the child about the here and now and what is going on about them. They modify their speech and interaction overall with great sensitivity as they try to keep the child's attention.

It is when the child starts to look at objects or events around them that the adult is stimulated to name and comment on these things (Gowen et al., 1992). Adults follow the child's focus of attention, attuning their speech to the child's interest. The adult's style is conversational, responding very positively to any response the child makes and working to keep the conversation going by deliberately passing turns to the child. In short, mothers interpret any signals the child makes, giving them meaning and then making judgements, based on their understanding of what the child is communicating. In all of this they are heavily dependent on feedback from the child; for example, eye gaze indicating attention, stilling of movements indicating listening, cooing indicating 'saying something'. Clearly, without these signals, the mother would find it hard to keep a flow of communication going; her timing would suffer so that she would stop and start uncertainly or conduct a one way flow of language at the child, thus abandoning the conversational style.

## The Developmental Pattern in Autism

Children with autism frequently show only a limited interest in faces and often seem to prefer gazing at objects, such as wheels, or lines. The lack or disturbance of eye contact is an obvious feature of their behaviour. For example, it can be fleeting, or actively avoided (Hutt and Ounsted, 1966; O'Connor and Hermelin, 1963). The effect of this is that the child fails to give the subtle, yet powerful, eye contact signals that the mother needs to build a flow of communication. This lack of response may in turn discourage the mother. In addition, the child's failure to see acts of communication by the mother as such, further limits the developmental pattern.

Children with autism often appear unaware of when they are being spoken to, apparently managing to sustain the focus of their attention on a self-selected task despite persistent attempts to engage them in the kind of 'conversations' described in the previous section. This lack of interest in speech makes it difficult for the parent to remain motivated to engage the child as readily and frequently as they would otherwise.

Although children with autism often make vocalisations or produce words, these can lack the quality of being a shared activity, often appearing to be for the child only. Such children may be silent for long periods but most use loud cries to signal distress or anger. The mother's instinct to limit such distress is powerful and quickly leads her to stop whatever she believes to be the cause. This can lead quickly to the child being 'left in peace'. These children also usually have a limited range of facial expressions, often appearing blank and smiling infrequently (Hermelin and O'Connor, 1985). This lack of feedback can be very disconcerting in that it is hard to know whether the interaction is pleasing the child or not. Remembering that mothers normally work hard to give meaning to responses, neutral expressions are quickly interpreted as signals of boredom and this inevitably impacts on the mothers' feelings.

Further, while children with autism may lead adults by the hand to objects they want, they rarely do so using eye contact, and finger pointing is often absent or infrequent (Hermelin and O'Connor, 1985). This lack of pointing means that the mother is not stimulated into the naming objects in the usual way. Also, the children have a limited motivation to imitate, or seem to do so with little understanding of how this could help establish communication. In addition to all of this, such children may find it hard to tolerate physical proximity; this is an important feature of the pattern when considering that most early communication happens at close range.

The reality of the above description is that the behaviour of the child with autism seems designed to switch off communication rather than stimulate it in the way which was described earlier. To exacerbate the problem, the child is growing and size is critical in triggering modifications to interaction and language. There is a sense in which adults cannot help changing the way in which they interact in that they are adapting as a natural response to the signals the child is giving. The adults are, therefore, doing what comes naturally (Berger and Cunningham, 1981; Buckhalt et al., 1978; Marfo, 1989).

However, the nature of the child's difficulty means that those involved will have to change this natural way of responding. This required change conflicts with what seems natural in the circumstances and so can be difficult to achieve; it may feel awkward and unsatisfactory. Conviction, enthusiasm and the support of family, friends and colleagues is needed, for invariably results come slowly. All involved must become adept at spotting small steps forward and so bring into play their skills at modifying and adapting to the child's responses. If a realistic understanding of how communication usually develops can be combined with an understanding of the disturbances which arise from autism, it is possible to develop strategies for keeping the process on track, introduce techniques to minimise the disturbance, and give this group of children access to the necessary learning experiences. These interactive processes of communication must underpin early speech development if the children are to learn meaningful communicative skills.

## Developing a Remedial Communication Programme

In conducting these remedial processes it is essential to work in partnership with parents. However, it is important to recognise that parents have already established a pattern of interaction with their child and although they may want to change it to help their child, to do so will require both courage and will-power in the face of the resistance that the child may seem to readily and persistently put forward. Parents will receive few instant rewards and this can be hard to bear.

One way forward is to teach the child a skill which the adult can recognise as a social interaction signal, such as giving eye contact when greeted, and to which parents can instantly and enthusiastically respond. The knowledge, that much of communication will follow automatically if the right signals are seen, should be remembered and used. In this way previously established patterns can begin to change with all parties recognising (at some level) successes and gradually building new skills. The fact that change is difficult for everyone should be acknowledged but small successes that are overtly discussed and which trigger parents' innate responsiveness, should help establish the confidence needed to take the risks involved. These processes of change apply equally to others working with the child who may not have considered the need to address problems with communication in this way; indeed the importance of considering the whole communication environment of the child is paramount.

In formulating a structured approach, there are some key principles that need to be applied. The aim is to increase the children's experience of social interaction and communication at a level from which they can learn core skills. This can be achieved through modifying aspects of the child's behaviour, modifying the way in which adults use their innate skills, and creating an awareness of environmental factors that can help or hinder these objectives.

## Developing signals that encourage communication

Each child needs to be observed carefully to gain a true understanding of what signals he/she is giving and the impact these have on those around. A careful evaluation of potential distractions in various settings is also needed. For example, some children find lines fascinating, so, attempting conversation in front of venetian blinds can be doomed to failure. Teaching may need to start at the very basic level of increasing the child's tolerance of being near adults. One parent observed that, 'half the problem with getting anything across to my son is that when you walk into a room he usually walks out'. Observation showed that the problem stemmed from an intolerance of doors being closed. This was worked on in the little group setting and, when successful there, was tackled at home. This meant the child was now more likely to be near adults and increased his opportunities for interaction. In addition, the parents felt their son was no longer avoiding them and this increased their confidence.

In the same vein, all the children at the little group are taught to sit in a circle or at a table and to remain seated while an adult leads an activity. The activity must be appealing so there is a real purpose for the child in being there. This involves persistence and undaunted enthusiasm from the adults. We know that children with autism do not always want to come, or to stay once brought, but with overt praise for 'good sitting' and a selection of toys likely to appeal, it is possible.

The children can be taught to tolerate closer physical proximity providing it has a meaningful purpose – perhaps to receive a tickle; to be helped into a box for a game of 'jack in the box', or to have their hand shaken with great enthusiasm in a greeting song. Again, the adult must ensure the activity has impact and appeal for the child. Whatever the context the question asked should be: 'Is the child close enough to be easily involved?'. If the answer is negative, then the teacher or parent needs to find ways to bring the child into closer proximity.

Eye contact is a very important way of signalling and this must be taught directly to children with autism, although it is important to recognise that the child will find such learning difficult. The need to look must be given a real purpose if a meaningful skill is to result. This may involve creating the need to look or developing any existing skills. This can be done at a basic level by always holding objects that you know the child wants right in front of your eyes and continuing to do this over a period of time until the child automatically looks up when they want something. This skill does move into eye to eye contact if the object is gradually held close to but not in front of the eyes and the child is always rewarded by clear praise, both verbal and facially expressed, plus the object of desire. This objective is easily followed up in activities which have pieces to be slotted into trays or put in boxes. The adult takes possession of all the pieces and only gives one to the child when they look at it as the adult is holding it close to their eyes.

Children can be taught to give eye contact when leading the adult to an object by building in a step whereby the child is helped to look at the adult before they step forward in the desired direction. In a similar way, familiar games can be made to grind to a halt so the child must give eye contact in order to trigger a continuation or 'more'. It is important to remember, here, that expectations must be realistic with all progress greeted with enormous approval, in recognition that the children are learning something that they find hard.

If a child can learn a greeting and respond to their name, they are multiplying their communication opportunities many times over. These early skills also put adults and peers at ease. The first stage is to see at what level the child currently gives or receives a greeting – can they give eye contact, make a 'thumbs up' sign, face the person, repeat hello if it is said first, shake hands and sing a hello song, or greet in a mature way but need help to know when it is appropriate? The need for a greeting has to be structured also, at least at the start of a session. In the little group each child is greeted before they can get into the classroom (many would walk in and take up with a favoured task without reference to the people around, if allowed). It is important to remember to make your greeting worth having – it must be enthusiastic, interesting facially as well as verbally, and it must be unfailingly persistent in the face of apparent lack of interest.

More complex greetings can be taught in conjunction with songs: for example, a short 'hello' song that each child sings to the next child in a circle, can be a natural progression. Each child is given whatever help is needed by the supporting adults. The target for a particular child may be to stand facing a peer receiving the greeting, to tolerate holding hands, to give eye contact, to actually shake the hand, to stay standing until the greeting is finished, or to sing the song solo. It is important that natural adult responsiveness should support each child appropriately and lead them forward in small steps.

Teaching children to respond to their name can be tackled in steps. First, it is important to call the child by name, even when nearby, and to expect a response – as opposed to leading them and saying their name simultaneously. It is also important to ensure that it is as easy as possible for the child to make eye contact, and that such contact is clearly given, even if at this stage it is not reciprocated. It may then help to call the child from a distance with an additional adult available to help the child focus on the person calling and then to prompt the child to head off in the right direction, thus giving the call a purpose.

Many other skills also need to be taught to the child in these careful small stages. These include interest in sounds and in faces, tolerance of the adult agenda, toleration of new experiences, imitation of, and responsiveness to, gestures, anticipation of events, turn taking, and the use of body posture to signal involvement. The skills described are regarded as central to all aspects of intervention. There is nothing revolutionary about any particular one but, providing they are tackled consistently, in small steps, children can move forward in their learning.

## Modifying the adult's communication skills

It is useful to take maximum advantage of the adult's inherent skills and abilities. For example, the ability to adapt, following feedback, can be utilised, providing the signals the child does give are recognised and interpreted accurately. It is also necessary to be aware of the impact the child might have on the manner of interaction. In this way adults can establish strategies to limit the impact of a child's disturbed signals and responses, thus limiting the disruption to the flow of communication.

It is also necessary to be aware of the child's level of attention, which can be prolonged for a task of their own choosing, while being minimal for an adult led task. An understanding of normal development helps, combined with a practical knowledge of each child. Certainly the therapeutic input must be presented as the most obvious source of stimulation for the child and the focus of attention must be intrinsic to a task or activity. This means working with a degree of aplomb and panache. New activities must be introduced with enthusiasm, with the adult clearly modelling that the task is fascinating and desirable. This can be wearing on the adult who seeks to work with the child but is necessary. It is frequently impossible to explain to the children that something is interesting, but it is possible to demonstrate interest and enthusiasm. There needs to be a clear understanding of what level of attention skill the child is being expected to achieve. For some children this may be that they look before averting their eyes or that they watched the adult take a turn before they take theirs; for others it may be that the child can watch for the duration of an activity.

There must be an understanding of the child's existing communication skills so that the adults' responsiveness can be used in each learning experience. This important evaluation can involve looking for very small signals. Can the child look at an object and then up to an adult? Does the adult have to be both close and at the same eye level in order to receive eye contact? Can the child fill the pause that is their turn with an eye glance, whole body alertness, or a sound or word? To work forward from the child's current level of ability means ensuring those involved can identify the signals the child gives, and respond to them with praise and positive reinforcement while constantly encouraging the child to go a little further.

An example of this in practice is the small child who enjoyed wearing a particular hat. He would put on the hat and than stand near an adult giving no other signals but clearly expecting something to happen. His existing level of communication was evaluated as his realising that he needed to be near an adult but failing to appreciate that he had more to do. The next step was identified; he should reach out to the adult and give eye contact, in order to trigger the adult into comments on the hat. The adult would than respond enthusiastically. For a verbal child the next step might have been to prompt and reward the child for saying 'look at me!'.

It is important to remember how new or inexperienced communicators need help, encouragement and prompting to fill the gap that is their turn in the conversation or interaction. It is all too easy to make the child's response for them, only ask questions that do not need a reply or generally sweep the activity on without a clear gap for the child's response. Recalling how hard mothers work at passing the turn to a baby in early interaction makes it clear that at least as much, and usually more, effort will be needed with children with autism. It is essential to be highly responsive if the child does anything that could constitute a response at the level that is individually targeted. For example, many children will still their body movements after a tickle, hoping that it will happen again. Providing that the pause for this to happen is created, and the response acknowledged and built on through the adult saying, 'you want MORE?', the beginnings of the turn taking, that is fundamental to the conversational style of interaction, can start.

More able children can be encouraged to accept role reversal in all games where they have been on the receiving end, thus giving them the chance to be the initiator. For instance, in a game where the adult has put the child into a pretend bed, sung them to sleep, and then woken them up with shouts of 'wake up', the adult should then get into the 'bed', hand the blanket to the child and help them take the commanding role. Use of these strategies can build active participation in situations where there is turn taking and create a genuine flow that is shared between adult and child.

Equally important is the need to look carefully and work out whether a behaviour is inappropriately taking the place of communication signals. This can be the case for children who require or provoke physical handling. The handling itself can become the focus of the child's attention, therefore effectively removing the need for, or complicating, any other response.

## Adult use of language

Adults need to keep their utterances short and work to overcome their tendency to use more mature language levels in relation to the size of the child. If adults do this, they automatically reduce grammatical complexity, so anxiety about exactly which grammatical features should be modified is not necessary. Also, research with language disordered children has suggested that sentence length is a critical factor in giving a child the chance to process what is being said (Wiig and Semel, 1984). Although there is some variation in the sentence lengths recommended, between 5–10 words seems an average target. Grammatically correct sentences rather than telegrammatic speech are used. With practice this skill can develop into fluent speech but initially it requires concentration. However, it is an important technique that can be used in most settings, and can work, as long as there is an acceptance that no one gets it right every time.

One strategy for controlling sentence length is to use pauses to break up an utterance into short chunks. There is a problem with this, however, in that there is a temptation to fill the pause with a quick aside. While utterances should be short, effort must also be made to keep the flow going by exaggerating the intonation patterns and playing on the rhythmic quality of some phrases. Mothers do this and it is known to help fix a child's attention span (Snow, 1986). This does not mean seesawing up and down in pitch range, but rather that underlying or existing patterns should be exaggerated. For example an 'oh NO' is delivered emphatically on a falling intonation, while a balloon being pumped up can be accompanied by cries of 'up up up' on a rising intonation. It is not necessary to plan the intonation patterns in advance; simply allow oneself to dramatise the patterns that come naturally in the circumstances.

We need to repeat words that we want a child to hear and understand. In the little group target words are repeated up to ten times before it is considered that the child has had a fair chance of understanding. This may seem both onerous and potentially boring for the adult but it need not be if, objects are named each time they are used, if when working in the group each child is told what to do before their turn, or if songs are used to give structure and momentum to games. It is a question of manipulating the activity to ensure that repetition of the key words or phrases is intrinsic to the flow of the game. For example, in a task where the child is being encouraged to squeeze dough, the following script can be brought to bear: Adult taking dough: 'I'm going to squeeze it' (while squeezing dough): 'SQUEEZE'. Then squeezing the dough repeatedly in time to singing to the tune of 'row, row, row the boat . . .', i.e. 'squeeze, squeeze, squeeze the play dough squeeze, squeeze, squeeze the play dough . . . now I'll give some to you!'. Then, on giving some to a child, take his or her hand containing the dough and squeeze it together: 'squeeze'. In this way, nine repetitions are achieved, and all before the adult has given another child some playdough following the same formula.

Equally, every effort should be made to keep language, focused clearly on the equipment being used, the activity being played or, for the more verbal child, the relevant topic. Learning to do this, requires concentration. Adults find it hard to resist sneaking in conversational asides, or striking up conversations with others, particularly as the child may not be giving much feedback. However, it is essential to bring this area of language use under control, and, in doing so, this will help the children focus on what is being said. Verbal messages must be obvious and relevant and, therefore, they should not be confused with background noise or talk. Facial expressions and gestures should be made clearly and held for longer than is usual in non-autistic interactions if the child is to have time to focus attention on the adult.

The child needs positively to look, if they are to begin to understand that a message is being signalled and that it means something. Pulling faces can be incorporated into games and songs. For example, the song, 'If you're happy and you know it' can be usefully employed to give a context to early imitation games. 'If you're happy and you know it go poohee/yuck/yummy' can be great fun providing all the adults join in with exaggerated responses! In addition to encouraging imitation, this game ensures appropriate labels are give to each expression.

**Appropriate language demands**

In addition to all the preceding targets, there need to be established goals for the level of language demand to be made on each child in order to ensure that the adults can stimulate the child to use their language skills at an optimum level and move forward. For some children this may mean identifying a core vocabulary that will be structured into the tasks or ensuring that the need to make a sign or gesture is essential for the child to achieve something that motivates them. For more able children it is possible to highlight particular grammatical structures through careful task manipulation and awareness of objectives.

Speech and language therapists can use their skills to observe all activities the child is involved with and identify ways in which communication objectives can become an intrinsic part of what the child is learning. They can also actively model communication at the level required for each child and observe and feed back to others information regarding what is actually happening in the communication process. In this way skills that are a genuine part of the child's life are taught and thus practice is more likely to occur at the level of repetition required to establish lasting skills.

## Modifications to the Environment

The best laid plans and therapeutic strategies can go wrong, especially in autism. However, it is possible to try and limit problems by looking at the setting for the intervention. This requires a pragmatic evaluation of any factors competing for the child's attention. Many individuals with autism report that focusing attention in visually distracting settings is difficult (Grandin, 1995; Williams, 1996). A general rule is that the overall context should be simplified as far as possible. There needs to be a constant monitoring of the level of visual and auditory stimulation in the room. Visual displays are kept colourful but simple. Displays that involve twirling three-dimensional lines and such like are avoided as these can be very difficult to compete with.

Similarly, visitors, although welcome, are asked to follow the focus of attention that is being modelled for the child and not to ask questions or to talk to each other while a session is in progress. This is very important for not only does it give clear messages about an important strategy but it reduces the amount of background noise that competes for the child's attention.

Routines to help build sequences are used, for example, overalls are put on before painting. These procedures make it easier to ensure communication demands at an appropriate level are built into the task. The quantity of equipment should be limited, as too many things on a table can make it hard to focus on one alone, and many toys on the floor can make a distractingly complex background against which to work. At the little group there is also an insistence on changes in the toys available; there are days when no trains are available, for example, so that children who find these hard to ignore are obliged to look elsewhere.

Children with autism need to be helped to work through whole tasks: to start, to do, and to finish, followed by, for example, replacing the toys in the appropriate place. This helps children move on from playing with only one aspect of a toy or from using materials inappropriately.

There are many other modifications that can be brought into use as needed, for example, techniques for behaviour management that focus on praise for co-operation at whatever level the child is expected to achieve, with undesirable behaviour receiving a minimum of stimulation. Always essential are clear objectives and the ability to work very closely as a team. Through working in close partnership with specialist teachers it has been possible in the little group to create a clear and consistent structure. Combined with this structure there is consistency in behaviour management with clear rules and expectations.

There is also an overall timetable so children can understand what will happen before they have the skills to follow verbal explanations. The elements of the approach outlined above can be formed into a structured programme that has sufficient flexibility to operate in all settings with some adaptation. Parents need to be involved early on, and, at all times, the goal of functional social communication should be built in to all interaction possibilities with the child.

## Evaluating the Results

Any evaluation of the impact of an approach relies on feedback from the parents and involved professionals and on careful observations of the children (Wiig and Semel, 1984). As yet no formal evaluation procedures have been undertaken at the little group. Until such time, the assessment of results is necessarily subjective but it is possible to observe children making progress in the development of eye contact patterns, tolerance of adult demands and proximity, and the ability to use communication signals to engage adults. It is also possible to observe the emergence of words or the use of signs that can be understood in terms of their place in the development of social interaction.

Many problems do, of course, persist, but the principles and techniques give all involved with the child an understanding of what needs to happen in the development of the child's communication. For those working with children with autism there are clear and definite benefits from the use of a programme that has small carefully graded steps that fit into an overall structure. Knowing what is to be done and why, helps engender confidence and this makes it easier to focus energy into constructive input rather than into generalised concerns.

This kind of approach allows each adult to use materials or activities they like, thus making it easier to create a rewarding time for all. The children enjoy the experiences and the rewards keep adults motivated in an area where the children's difficulties make serious demands on this motivation. Such an approach as described provides a structure that includes small steps in development that can be sensitised on an individual basis while allowing those involved with the children to utilise their innate communication skills, and to work with enthusiasm, humour and verve in encouraging the children to develop to their full potential.

# References

Berger J.& Cunningham C.C., (1981) 'The development of eye contact between mothers and normal versus Down's syndrome infants'. *Developmental Psychology*, **17**, 5, 678–689.

Brooks-Gunn J. & Lewis M., (1984) 'Maternal responsivity in interactions with handicapped infants'. *Child Development*, **55**, 3, 782–793.

Bruner, J. (1975) 'The ontogenesis of speech acts'. *Journal of Child Language, 2,* 1–20

Buckhalt J.A. Rutherford R.B. & Goldberg K.E., (1978) 'Verbal and non-verbal interaction of mothers with their Down's syndrome and non-retarded infants'. *American Journal of Mental Deficiency, 82*, 4, 337–343.

Butterworth, G. (1991) 'The ontogeny and phylogeny of joint visual attention', in A. Whiten (ed.) *Natural Theories of Mind.* Oxford: Blackwell.

Clarkson M.G. & Berg W.G. (1983) 'Cardiac orienting and vowel discrimination in newborns: crucial stimulus parameters'. *Child Development, 54*, 1, 162–171.

Crnic, K.A., Rgozin, A.S., Greenberg, M.T., Robinson, N. M. & Basham, R.B. (1983) 'Social interaction and developmental competence on pre-term and full-term infants during the first year of life'. *Child Development, 54*, 5, 1199–1210.

Cross, T.G. (1977) 'Mothers' speech adjustments: the contributions of selected child listener variables', in C.E. Snow and C.A. Ferguson (eds) *Talking to Children: Language Input and Interaction.* Cambridge: Cambridge University Press.

Gowen, J.W., Johnson-Martin, N., Golmann, B.D. & Hussey, B. (1992) 'Object play and exploration in children with and without disabilities: a longitudinal study'. *American Journal of Mental Retardation, 97*, 1, 21–38.

Grandin, T. (1995) 'How people with autism think', in E. Schopler & G.B. Mesibov (eds) *Learning and Cognition in Autism.* New York: Plenum Press.

Hermelin, B. & O'Connor, N. (1985) 'Logico-affective states and non-verbal language', in E. Schopler & G.B. Mesibov (eds) *Communication Problems in Autism.* New York: Plenum Press.

Hutt, C. & Ounsted, C. (1966) 'The biological significance of gaze diversion with particular reference to the syndrome of infantile autism'. *Behavioural Sciences,* **11**, 346–356.

Jordan, R.R. (1993) 'The nature of the linguistic and communication difficulties of children with autism', in D. Messer & G. Turner (eds) *Critical Influences on Language Acquisition and Development.* London: Macmillan.

Kaye K. (1979) 'Thickening thin data: the maternal role in developing communication and language', in M. Bullowa (ed.) *Before Speech.* Cambridge: Cambridge University Press.

Kaye, K. (1982) *The Mental and Social Life of Babies.* London: Methuen.

Marfo, K. (1989) 'Maternal directiveness in interactions with mentally handicapped children: an analytical commentary'. *Journal of Child Psychology and Psychiatry,* **31**, 531–549.

Murray, L. and Trevarthen, C. (1986) 'The infants role in mother-infant communications', *Journal of Child Language,* **13** 15–29.

O'Connor, N. & Hermelin, B. (1963) 'Measures of distance and mobility in psychotic children and severely subnormal controls'. *British Journal of Social and Clinical Psychology,* **3**, 29–33

Smith, B.R. and Leinonen, E. (1992) *Clinical Pragmatics. Unravelling the Complexities of Communicative Failure.* London: Chapman and Hall.

Snow, C. (1972) 'Mothers' speech to children learning language'. *Child Development,* **42**, 549–565.

Snow, C. (1977) The development of conversation between mothers and babies', *Journal Child Language,* **4**, 1–22.

Snow, C. (1986) 'Child directed speech', in P. Fletcher & M. Garman (eds) *Language Acquisition: Studies in First Language Development,* 2nd edition. Cambridge: Cambridge University Press.

Stern, D.N. (1974) 'Mother and infant at play: the dyadic interaction involving facial, vocal and gaze behaviours', in M. Lewis & L.A. Rosenblum (eds) *The Effects of the Infant on its Caregiver.* New York: Wiley.

Trevarthen, C., Aitken, K., Papoudi, D. & Robarts, J. (1996) *Children with Autism: Diagnosis and Interventions to Meet their Needs.* London: Jessica Kingsley.

Wasserman, G.A., Allen, R. & Linares, L.O., (1988) 'Maternal interaction and language development in children with and without speech related anomalies'. *Journal of Communication Disorders,* **21**, 4, 319–333.

Wiig, E. & Semel, E. (1984) *Language Learning, Assessment and Intervention for the Learning Disabled.* 2nd edition. Columbus, OH: Charles E. Merrill.

Williams, D. (1996) *Autism: An Inside Out Approach.* London: Jessica Kingsley.

## COMMENTARY

When thinking of using a cognitive approach, practitioners sometimes imagine that it is only appropriate to the most able, or to those who have good language skills. In this chapter, Davies shows how we do not have to wait for the development of any 'entry' skills to adopt such an approach and that, indeed, the approach can be used in the development of those very language skills. As she says, she illustrates her approach with her work with pre-school children, but it would be equally useful for older developmentally delayed (as well as autistic) children and adults and the principles underlying it could be applied to developing communication even in those who already have structural language.

## The Transactional Nature of Teaching

One of the most important aspects of this work is its explicit recognition of the transactional nature of teaching and the use of the teacher's responses (as well as the child's) to further interaction. It is only through reflection on one's own reactions in a teaching situation that one is able to modify those reactions to create an environment that will benefit the child with autism. Davies illustrates very well how knowledge of normal developmental processes need to inform teaching but that such knowledge is not sufficient. The teacher must also be aware of the particular difficulties likely to arise in autism, and the specific difficulties faced by the particular individual, in order to adapt and build on those strategies that normally foster that development.

## Different forms of Communicative Discourse

It is also useful to have the clear exposition, in this chapter, of the fact that communication in the classroom is, nevertheless, still communication, and that the particular discourse style of didactic teaching is not the most useful way of beginning to teach communicative understanding. Thus, Davies recognises the need to teach communicative skills that will be useful in classroom situations (such as responsiveness to verbal instructions and social greetings) but the focus of her work is on teaching the early communicative exchanges that will help elucidate the process of communication itself for the child. Davies shows, for example, that it is more effective to build on the child's natural interests and focus of attention, rather than expecting the child to tune in to that of the adult. Communication skills are necessary for full access to the curriculum, as Davies recognises, but the first stage is to help the child understand the nature of communication in meaningful interactive routines. This point supports those made by Jordan and Libby (Chapter 3) in defending the role of play in the curriculum.

## Structured Communicative Exchanges

It is also interesting to see how a highly personal and affective interactional approach nevertheless can be approached in a structured way, to make it accessible to the child with autism. An important principle of that structure is that the child's spontaneous actions are given communicative import by the adult and the child is shown explicitly how to use and develop those actions within the interaction. The interaction is not expected to be meaningful in itself to the child with autism, so the interaction is always built around activities which do have an intrinsic meaning for the child. Important interaction skills, such as eye contact, are never taught in isolation, but always as part of a meaningful routine.

Part of the structure, also, involves ensuring that the child's difficulties do not create barriers to communication nor develop into secondary disabilities. Thus, Davies gives examples of ensuring that the child is physically able to tolerate situations in which interaction can occur, by identifying any barriers and teaching strategies to overcome these barriers. The use of music enhances the structure for the child and the adult's role is always a facilitatory one, allowing the child time and space to make a response, before intervening. The emphasis is on structure that supports the process of learning, rather than achieving set responses, and its success depends on the sensitivity of the adult in responding to each child's needs. Prompts are used where necessary, but the structure, the small steps, and, most importantly, the use of spontaneously motivating activities, help prevent the child becoming prompt dependent.

## Teaching as an Art

Strict behavioural approaches became popular in special education in the 1960s and 1970s because they seemed to offer both accountability (with clear measurable objectives) and a technique that could be used without professional knowledge or skill. Such approaches have fallen out of favour, as their limitations became apparent (Brechin and Walmsley,1989), but current emphases on measurable learning outcomes and teacher competencies are having similar effects in 'de-skilling' teachers (Jordan and Powell, 1995). It is encouraging to see the unashamed recognition, in this chapter, that teaching is not a technology that can simply apply learning theory in a pre-determined programme. Rather it involves working with 'aplomb and panache', demonstrating 'that the task is fascinating and desirable', being sensitive to the child's idiosyncratic signals and being an opportunist who can capitalise on each situation as it arises. None of this can be prescribed, but Davies is right in her appraisal. Teaching communication may involve behaviours that are normally seen in young infants, but that makes the task more, not less, difficult. It is a task that requires the highest degree of professional expertise and art.

# References

Brechin, A. & Walmsey, J. (1989) *Making Connections: Reflecting on the Lives and Experiences of People with Learning Difficulties.* London: Hodder and Stoughton/Open University Press.

Jordan, R.R. & Powell, S.D. (1995) 'Skills without understanding: a critique of a competency-based model of teacher education in relation to special needs'. *British Journal of Special Education,* **22**, 120–124.

# CHAPTER 10

# The development of the outdoor education programme at Storm House School

Geoff Evans

## Introduction

Prior to 1986, as at most schools for children with autism, our pupils had gone on walks, occasionally they had scrambled on local rocks and participated in the yearly 'holiday' to the seaside, which may have included some pursuit type activities. In 1986, our school experienced change. We had a new principal, quite a large number of new staff and we were starting to get a small number of referrals for children with Asperger's Syndrome. It was a good time to look at the curriculum we offered over the school's 24 hours. It was in these circumstances that teachers and residential staff looked for alternative ways of delivering the school's curriculum to our new pupils and also to our existing ones, many of whom were towards the lower end of the autistic continuum in terms of intellectual ability. Some also presented severely challenging behaviour.

Together with a teacher, Kit Howe, I started the adventure club which ran during the residential hours but also included selected day pupils. From the first meeting the club was a success. Pupils joined in enthusiastically with walks and short climbs, using equipment borrowed from Scout groups, friends and me (this is not recommended!). At the same time, two pupils were joining Wath Comprehensive School for outdoor pursuits on two days a week. Both pupils were excelling at climbing, abseiling, walking and gorge scrambling. Often it was noticed that their skills were equal, if not superior, to many of their peers.

Over the next year, with grants from the Sports Council and Yorkshire TV's Christmas appeal, we were able to buy our own equipment and so offer outdoor education to a much larger number of pupils. The only obstacle we met was the disbelief of some parents and staff that their children or pupils could actually do such things and a genuine doubt that they would enjoy it. There were also some feelings around about pupils being involved in dangerous activities. Slowly the pupils won everyone over by their achievements and often pure enjoyment of the activities.

After the first year, outdoor education was open to all. Most classes managed to go once a week, while the younger pupils enjoyed the occasional day out and a whole week each year of adventurous activities. As the school has grown, it has become impossible to give all the pupils the opportunity to engage in outdoor activities each week, and priority is now given to the older pupils. Residential pupils continue to have access to adventurous activities on a weekly basis in the summer months. When people see videos of our pupils engaging in outdoor activities, they often ask if these are our most able pupils. It is with some pride that I have said 'No, actually he has to be pushed around in a wheel chair at home, because he will not walk'. With amazement, they look once more at him half way up a 50 ft climb. It has always been that outdoor education is for all abilities, and that all usually benefit from it.

Over the last ten years, we have been able to expand the number of different activities that we offer our pupils from the initial walking and climbing, to a list that now includes: abseiling, canoeing, kayaking, gorge scrambling, dry slope skiing, mountain biking, adventure and problem solving games, and the occasional experience such as four wheel driving and caving.

## Why Outdoor Education with Pupils with Autism?

The simple answer is that, with the right support, they are good at it. It is something that they seem to take to, and for which in time are able to develop relevant skills. This could be because much of what we do is about an individual response to a problem, for example, climbing a rock, (though as you will see, this is not always true). Also, the use of language is limited and restricted to a few well chosen words when pupils are actually engaged in the activity. And again, the aims of most of our activities seem to be easily understood by the child with autism. For example, when climbing, you start at the bottom and continue until you reach the top, where you stop. Finally, I believe that working out of doors often gives our pupils the freedom and space that they need. For many this results in a lowering of the anxiety level.

Outdoor education, done well, seeks to develop the whole person, the intellect, body and emotions. Often the educational experience we offer our pupils seeks to just impart skill (often much needed) without recognising that, like us, the child with autism needs far more. Activities like adventure walking and problem solving games attempt to stretch the pupil physically, mentally and emotionally. With skilful and sensitive facilitation, outdoor education can give children insights into their own feelings and emotions. Many of our pupils lack the understanding necessary to identify what for us are basic emotions like fear, anxiety, joy and happiness. Over the past ten years, we have seen a number of pupils learn to identify the emotions, label them appropriately and then go on to learn to manage them.

The final reason is more simple; that outdoor education provides opportunities for staff and pupils to share in common experiences like getting wet, feeling tired, being scared together. With facilitation, the pupils and staff can learn much from each other and develop coping skills.

## The Aims of Outdoor Education at Storm House School

The aims of our programme have been developed over the years; they are explored in the sections below. It should be remembered that the activities are just vehicles through which the aims and objectives can be achieved.

### To provide an experience of a variety of outdoor activities

Most of our pupils fail at traditional games like football and tennis, very often because they fail to see the purpose of the game or to understand the sometimes complex rules. For these reasons, we seek to offer our pupils a wide range of activities that they can enjoy and succeed in. We try to offer a range of activities that are both land and water based. Most pupils are able to join in the activities without any adaptation or special equipment, but when necessary, the school tries to provide it, so that as many pupils as possible can join in together. For example, we provide tandem bikes for those pupils who cannot balance, steer and brake at the same time, or who have little road sense.

### To develop physical fitness

Few of our pupils had experienced sustained physical activity before they came to our school. Many came with a low level of fitness and, in particular, stamina. Through a structured programme of walks and other activities such as climbing and canoeing, pupils are able to significantly increase their level of fitness. Another of our aims in this area is to teach our pupils how to use their muscles effectively and appropriately. Some pupils lack the basic know-how of how to step up or to go under objects; at first their arms and legs seem to be working against them, rather than for them. With instruction and guidance, pupils are able to learn how to use their arms, legs and bodies effectively.

### To provide experiences of different environments

Either because of behaviour difficulties or an unwillingness to visit new places, many children with autism have a limited experience of the variety of different environments that surround them. Some have specific fears of features such as woods or open moors and such places are often intimidating or frightening to them. Throughout the programme, we seek to teach about, and enable the pupil to experience, a variety of environments including woodlands, expanses of water both natural and man made, open moors, valleys, hilltops, farming areas and also industrial areas close to the school. Through experiential learning, we seek to help the pupil feel more comfortable with them.

We also seek to teach the socially accepted behaviour for each environment. For example, you don't throw stones off the top of a cliff, but it is acceptable to skim stones across an expanse of water. On all our field trips, a great emphasis is placed upon teaching the pupils the relevant codes and rules. For example, we teach the country code. Emphasis is also placed upon conserving the environment and trying to help our pupils appreciate its fragility.

## To learn group skills and encourage co-operation between pupils

The outdoor programme gives pupils the opportunity to work together with other pupils to solve problems or simply to have a good time. Activities such as Canadian canoeing encourage pupils to work and communicate together in order to navigate the canoe around the lake. Group games like spiders web (the object is to get all the group through the 'web' without touching it) have proven useful for learning about being part of a group. Lessons learnt in such games have been applied to group living in the residential provision. This aim is relevant to all pupils with autism, perhaps more so to those who are more able, but find it difficult to function in, or understand, groups.

## For pupils to learn about their own feelings and emotions

Very often the teaching of children with autism has concentrated on the imparting of knowledge and skills. Of equal importance for some is enabling them to understand and manage their feelings and emotions. Involvement in adventurous activities involves so many feelings and emotions, that it makes a good vehicle for teaching pupils about them. Prior to understanding and managing emotions, is recognising them as Sinclair (1992) has noted. Many pupils know that they are experiencing something, but often lack the vocabulary to express these feelings. We have done much work on helping pupils to recognise, label and express the emotions experienced when engaged in such activities as climbing. For example, one young man used to shout, 'I don't like jacket potatoes' when halfway up a climb. This was his way of expressing anxiety. In the past, he had found jacket potatoes hard to cut and eat, and now he was applying that experience to another difficult situation. Over a period of time we were able to teach him to recognise the changes in his body and use appropriate expressions for these feelings.

## To give opportunities to learn new skills

Each activity has its own skills that must be mastered in order for success to be experienced. Some skills are obvious, such as putting on a life jacket and using a paddle, while others are not so obvious, for example, maintaining personal safety, knowing when you are cold or tired. Each skill has to be identified, analysed, taught and constantly reinforced.

### To enjoy the activity and experience success

This is the final aim, but is as important as those above, even more so for some pupils. Enjoyment and success do not come naturally to our pupils; they need to be taught about them and encouraged to experience them. Pupils' feelings of success and enjoyment are often dependent upon those of the staff and how they communicate them. Some pupils have only learned to recognise success because staff have applauded them, told them what they have achieved, and praised them.

## Objectives of Outdoor Education

Within each of the aims above will be specific objectives in relation individuals with autism.

### Development of the self

Outdoor pursuits can be used to develop a knowledge of the self (which Powell and Jordan (1993) suggest may be disturbed in autism), the exercise of self-control, and eventually self respect. Alongside this will come the development of the physical abilities, relevant skills, and appropriate communication to exercise this sense of self, In turn, this will lead to leadership skills, problem solving skills, and awareness of their own safety.

### Relating to the group

The programme involves taking part in planning, taking part in reviews, sharing leadership roles, supporting and helping others, encouraging others, and being aware of the safety of the group. Outdoor pursuits allows each of these issues to be taught directly in relevant contexts that have meaning for the child. It also fosters the enjoyment of being with others.

### Relating to the environment

Clearly, the programme helps the children become aware of many different environments, to learn to appreciate their different characteristics and to learn appropriate descriptive words (valley, cliff) to describe them. It also teaches them in a very practical way how their actions impact on that environment and how to protect the environment for the future.

## Selection of Activities

The selection of the right activity for pupils is as important in the outdoors as it is in the classroom, possibly more so, as a mistake in the classroom seldom results in serious injury to pupils. The factors below are those that are considered when selecting activities for inclusion in the programme.

### What are the benefits of this activity for the child with autism?

This ensures that activities have specific relevant objectives within the overall curriculum aims of the school, and that the specific learning needs of the pupils are addressed. Activities are sought that will encourage communication, problem solving and/or co-operation. The skills that are developed through the activity chosen should be such that they can be used in other situations with support.

### What are problems for children with autism?

Alongside the benefits that are expected, it is necessary for (often enthusiastic) staff to also appraise the activity for any potential difficulties that may arise. This does not necessarily mean that the activity will not be undertaken, but disadvantages have to be balanced against potential benefits and the appraisal gives an opportunity to develop ways of overcoming barriers or preventing possible difficulties from arising. Examples of potential difficulties are the distance to be travelled and whether the activity is in a noisy or crowded place.

### What are the risks involved?

The most important part of the appraisal of a task, however, is a risk-benefits analysis. If risks are identified (and few outdoor pursuits will be entirely risk free), staff have to consider whether such risks can be controlled and managed effectively. In other words, how safe can we make it for the pupil with autism? This question is best answered by carrying out a risk assessment of the environment, activity and the pupils involved.

One part of this assessment will be a consideration of whether the staff have the relevant qualifications to instruct the activity. The qualifications to instruct many outdoor activities such as climbing, canoeing and sailing are set by the sport's governing body. Experience is much harder to assess. My own feeling is that in order to work with children with autism, this experience should be built up over a number of years and should include working outdoors with them. This is particularly important because of their communication difficulties and the unpredictable behaviour of some. An anecdote may serve to illustrate the point that you can be qualified and experienced but still get into problems when working with children with autism if you do not understand the nature of their communication problems. I once heard a Canadian canoe instructor in the centre of a lake say, 'Okay, let's go to the side and get out'. Immediately the child with autism stood up, walked to the side of the canoe and got out into the water. This was no great problem as the child was wearing a life jacket, but it makes the point about understanding the communication problems.

### Fun and challenge

When selecting activities for our outdoor education programme, we attempt to choose activities that are fun but also challenge the pupils mentally, physically and emotionally. Getting the balance right between fun and challenge is very important. If an activity is all fun, it can soon fall apart and result in behaviour management problems. Yet, if the challenge is too great, this can be too much for the child with autism and can result in withdrawal or challenging behaviour. Each activity offers something for the pupil to learn and experience. Canoeing can enable pupils to experience that calm sensation of gliding over the water, while climbing lets the pupils experience fear, excitement and the final relief of reaching the top.

## Benefits

The following is an outline of some of our activities, which shows how our pupils can benefit from them.

### Canoeing

Most pupils seem to benefit from canoeing simply by just being in the canoe and enjoying the motion caused by being on the water. This should not be minimised, particularly for those pupils whose lives are full of anxiety and stress. Others have learnt the basic skills required to take a kayak around an inland lake safely and in control. As stated earlier, some pupils have practised and developed their communication skills by paddling a Canadian canoe with another pupil. Finally, canoeing is fun and enjoyable, particularly on a hot summer's day. Such situations can show the child with autism that learning can be enjoyable, both for them and adults.

### Rock climbing

This was one of our first activities and has remained very popular with pupils of all abilities. This is possibly due to the fact, mentioned earlier, that its aims are easily understood by the pupil with autism. It can be a solitary activity: you and the rock. Many of the climbs that are popular with our pupils follow an obvious line or crack. In many ways, climbing is the perfect activity for our pupils, and it is no surprise to me that they do so well at it. While the above is true, we must not forget the constant problem solving that takes place when climbing, and the many occasions when pupils have to listen, understand and act upon instructions.

### Adventure walking

These walks take place over a full day and incorporate a number of activities and problem solving exercises. During the walk, the pupils may be required to squeeze between two rocks, crawl for a few yards through a rock tunnel, traverse on low rocks, find objects or navigate from one point to another. These are usually exciting and exhilarating days for both pupils and staff.

They are also days when a skilled instructor or teacher can facilitate much learning. Staff will be continually looking for ways of enabling the pupils to solve their own problems rather than giving solutions and answers. When a pupil is struggling on a rock traverse, it is tempting to say, 'Put your left hand here, your right foot there'. It is much harder to encourage the pupil to look, feel, and experiment until he or she finds the correct hold or move. We are consistently trying to give pupils confidence in their own abilities, rather than reinforcing the idea that the teachers have all the answers.

Adventure walks can be as complex or as simple as we wish. The important factors are: that pupils are fully involved and not just followers, as on many walks, that the activities and walk challenge the pupils but do not put them off by being too long or too hard and that the activities have a purpose and complement each other. The purpose may be as simple as teaching pupils to follow directions such as over, under or through. Or it may be more complex like map reading or decision making.

## Photo expeditions

The object of this activity is to select a subject and then photograph it. All that is needed is a map, a camera or preferably a selection of different cameras, a large number of films, photograph albums and a form of transport. Recent subjects in our residential department have been buildings and forms of transport. The obvious learning outcomes are learning to use a camera, selecting what to photograph and learning to use a map for the selection of locations. Less obvious outcomes are helping the pupils make decisions, negotiate over which venue to visit and learn to focus and look at an object or scene, something our pupils find difficult without a camera.

## Residential experiences

Over the years, the field trip or residential experience has made a considerable contribution to our outdoor education programme. These weeks away have taken place in many parts of this country and once in France. Our main venues have been the Lake District, Wales, the Peak District and the Yorkshire Dales. Most programmes, especially in recent years have been a mixture of adventurous and cultural activities. Residentials are something that most schools offer, so I have gone into more details concerning the programmes and their benefits.

It may be an obvious statement, but the more the pupils are involved in the residential, the more they benefit from it. Involvement starts with the preparation: writing to tourist boards, helping to book accommodation, planning the route. The most benefit has come from being involved in the selection of activities for the programme. Of course there are always weird and wonderful suggestions like deep sea diving and parachuting, but even these can be used to facilitate learning. Pupils are encouraged through discussion and negotiation to select activities that fit the following criteria:

1. It is of interest to more than one member of the group.
2. It is available in the area we are going to visit.
3. We have the staffing and expertise to do the activity.
4. It is within the budget.
5. We can do it safely.

Such decisions are not easy for our pupils, particularly as they may be making decisions from limited information and about places they have not been to. With careful guidance, such planning sessions can be very helpful to pupils in developing decision making, negotiating, communication and group work skills. The residentials are wonderful opportunities for pupils to learn to generalise the skills they have been learning for the past year. They also provide opportunities to learn how to adapt skills and behaviour to different social settings. For example, they include washing up, bathing and taking a shower. But, with the right level of support, the skills are very soon re-established and often strengthened because of the opportunities to generalise. While the occasional pupil has not responded to the opportunities presented, overall, the residential has been a time of accelerated learning.

## A Short Evaluation of the Outdoor Education Programme

This evaluation does not make any scientific claims. It is simply the observations of someone involved in outdoor education with children with autism over a ten-year period. The initial reasons for choosing to work out of doors with children with autism were simple; they enjoyed it and seemed to be good at it. This reason still stands today, particularly as many people are beginning to realise the importance of enjoyment and having fun in the education of children with autism (Jordan and Powell, 1995). Some of our pupils have continued to achieve reasonable skill levels in climbing and canoeing and more recently, skiing. The acquisition of skills has never been a major aim of ours, but it is still very rewarding to see the smile of satisfaction on pupils' faces when they master a canoeing stroke or learn to use a piece of equipment appropriately. Pupils' general level of fitness has increased over the years, as has their control over their own bodies through activities like weaselling (crawling between rocks and through gaps). But the major benefits for our pupils have been in personal development. Some of these benefits are outlined below.

### Growth in confidence

Many pupils with autism are lacking in confidence, particularly in relation to physical activities and their own bodies. This may be due to the limited opportunities to experience success physically. Over very short periods of time, we have seen pupils learn to be more at ease and in control of their bodies. This has led to a greater confidence in their abilities and willingness to attempt new activities. One young man came to our school a number of years ago, totally lacking in physical confidence, so much so that he would not even walk down short slopes. After many years of building up his confidence and physical skills, he has recently learnt how to ski. While we cannot prove that confidence gained through outdoor education generalises to other aspects of the pupil's life, we have certainly seen complementary development.

## Awareness of self

Traditionally we have taught awareness of self through the use of mirrors, photographs and now videos. Through outdoor education, many pupils have started to be aware of themselves first physically and then as a person who can make decisions and solve problems. One boy on his first walk with us, bumped into trees and walked precariously close to the edge of cliffs without any awareness of the dangers. Within four months, the same boy was not only avoiding trees and edges, but, when gorge scrambling, he was hopping from boulder to boulder and ducking under branches.

## Development of emotional awareness

Most of us know when we are afraid, scared and at our emotional limits, and we usually find the appropriate words to express our feelings. In similar circumstances, many of our pupils engage in bizarre behaviour or even severe challenging behaviour because of this lack of ability to identify their problem, talk about it or find a solution to it. Through the use of activities like climbing, problem solving games and gorge scrambling, some pupils have learnt to identify, label and manage emotions. This for some has been a slow process, sometimes over a number of years, but, by asking questions like: 'Are your legs shaky?'. 'Does your tummy feel tight?' 'Are you sweating?', we have been able to help the pupils identify and name anxiety and fear. Once they have reached that stage, it was much easier for them to make a decision about going up a climb or leading a group, for example.

## Co-operation with others

I have already referred to the use of problem solving games and canoeing to achieve co-operation with others. The preparation and planning stages of activities are also important. Often in the residential provision, four pupils all want to do a different outdoor activity. Staff have become quite skilled at enabling them as a group to look at all the factors involved and sometimes to give and take.

**Ability to reflect on experiences**

Successful completion of an activity is not the only result that we are looking for at the end of the day of climbing with children with autism. Hopefully the child will have learnt many other things during the rock climb. For example, they may have waited patiently for their go, co-operated in putting on the harness, expressed fears, overcome anxiety, followed instructions, distinguished between reaching with right or left hands. Central to reinforcing and enabling further learning is the ability to reflect on what you have done.

Reflection does not come easily to the child with autism (Powell and Jordan, 1992) and usually has to be taught if it is to be constructive. Reflection is best encourage immediately after the activity by such questions as, 'What did you do?' 'Who helped you?' 'How did you do it?'. Questions about the physical experience are also important, for example, 'Did your legs shake?' 'Were you smiling?' 'Did your hands sweat?'. On returning to school, other staff are encouraged to ask similar questions. This is often done quite naturally within our school. Yet further reinforcement is given when the video and photographs are ready, and staff will talk through them with pupils. Staff are now becoming more aware of the importance of reflection in enabling pupils to learn from their experiences.

**Learning not to be dependant upon teachers or adults**

It is our hope in all the activities that pupils will eventually become as independent as possible, given the safety requirements of the activity. To facilitate this, pupils are enabled to understand problem solving and are taught practical strategies. They are also encouraged to practise these skills in a variety of situations and environments, until they can do so without prompts. We have recently seen some success with a group of key stage 3 pupils who, after a hesitant start, are putting a distance between themselves and staff, in order to solve their own problems. One boy was recently observed carrying out his own risk assessment of a problem, before confidently and successfully solving it.

**Learning to be safe**

Many children with autism have little sense of safety either for themselves or for others. It is not uncommon for pupils to push someone out of the way or to walk precariously close to the edge of a cliff. An important port of the programme has been to teach pupils basic safety awareness and skills. Pupils are enable to develop skills in the recognition of danger, its evaluation and ways of coping with the risk.

While steep cliffs and fast flowing rivers may be obvious hazards to us, it is not so for some of our pupils, who have had to be taught to recognise each hazard they encounter. Once a risk is recognised, it has to be evaluated. For example, what is the likelihood of an accident and how severe would it be? This is often done by discussion with the pupils and asking questions such as: 'Is it safe to walk there?'. 'What might happen if you slipped?'. 'Is the tree strong enough to hold your weight?'. 'What would happen to your body if you fell?'. The final step in the process involves making a judgement and controlling the risk. Pupils are then often asked to make a decision. Should they walk there, or somewhere else? Is there anything they could do to make it safer? To begin with there may need to be prompts, such as the suggestion that they wear a helmet or hold onto a rope, but gradually they begin to make their own suggestions. Sometimes the decision may be inappropriate, and put the pupil at risk. Then the process is explored again. If the answers are still the same, then staff do make the final decision, but with an explanation of why. Teaching pupils to be safe without total reliance upon staff is not easily achieved, but, if consistent and patient, staff can have success.

### Other outcomes

There are many other outcomes of involvement in outdoor education for pupils with autism. The following are just some of them. Pupils begin to recognise the needs of their own bodies for warmth and food, and that these needs change throughout the day in accordance to changes in the weather and environment. They also learn to follow instructions independently, or with minimum support from staff. They learn about the environment, through being able to identify landshapes and usage, and to see man's impact upon it. They learn about trees, flowers and animals. All this information can lead to greater appreciation of the outdoor environment and increase the enjoyment of it.

## Teaching Problem Solving Skills

This is a brief outline of one way in which we teach and enable our pupils to problem solve using a river crossing.

### Describe the problem

In describing the problem, we give only that information necessary to solve it. Too much information can confuse the pupils and too much help can limit their creativity and final achievement. Any restrictions need to be carefully described and introduced. For example, 'Don't get wet!'.

### Make the problem clear

Some pupils fail to recognise the problem or simply have no desire to solve it. Motivation can increase, once the problem is identified and pupils are helped to recognise that they can solve it.

### Demonstrate a method or approach to the problem

The timing of this is important. A small number of pupils have not been able to attempt a problem without first seeing someone else do it. More usually, demonstrations are used to refine problem solving skills and to present alternatives.

### Giving support and encouragement

Again timing is crucial if the pupils are to maximise their learning. It is very tempting to help a pupil who seems to be stuck on a rock, but waiting a short time can result in pupils taking a step towards solving it themselves or asking for help. The support can be physical or verbal.

### Accept all attempts and reward them

A hesitant attempt to place a foot on a rock can become a very confident one if the verbal reward is well timed.

### Help pupils to become aware of their success

Say what they have achieved. It may be appropriate to over-play your praise in order for them to realise their success.

### Encourage variation

If a pupil has crossed successfully in one area, encourage them to move to another that may present different problems.

### Increase difficulty

Introduce rules to make the problem more difficult; 'You must keep your feet dry'. 'You can only step on small rocks.', or limit the number of rocks that can be used.

### Reflection

To maximise learning, reflection should take place and include both the process and the feelings. By reflecting on the process, pupils can learn how to problem solve. Ask questions like: 'Which place did you consider crossing at and why?' 'What were the problems?'. 'How did you do it?'. 'How could you improve next time?'. Questions about feelings are very important for our pupils. What and how you ask it is dependant upon individual pupils, but we often ask questions about what is happening to the body and then explore appropriate emotions: 'Were you shaky?'. 'Can you think of a word to describe how you felt?', and so on. Maybe we would give pupils a list of emotions and enable them to select an appropriate one.

### Practise the skills

We have found it important to quickly reinforce success and build upon it by giving opportunities for practice. Equally important is not to overwork a new skill. The balance always has to be a matter of professional judgement.

### Encourage generalisation

Some pupils have been able with help to generalise the process they used in crossing the river to other situations. One young man, who sometimes became very angry when faced with a problem he found difficult to solve, successfully crossed a river calmly after many attempts. Through reflection, we were able to help him identify the process he used and how he could apply this to other situations. It did not solve all his problems, but it was another step on the way.

## Conclusions

The teaching and facilitating of outdoor education for pupils with autism involves far more than teaching facts, rules and procedures. It is also about teaching values, emotions, feelings, processing information and making decisions. All these can be difficult for our pupils but can be learnt with skilful facilitation from staff. There are a number of important factors which I identify in our approach.

The first point is that we start where the pupils are, accepting existing strengths and skills and building upon them. Secondly, we have tried to involve the whole person, not just their intellect, but also their emotional and physical feelings. We give pupils responsibility for themselves and others and staff have learnt to act as facilitators more than teachers. We do not rest on our laurels, but continually try new activities and develop our existing ones. We concentrate on the learning process more than the final outcomes and, related to this we attempt to make the activities a happy and fun experience while still making them safe. We have high expectations of our pupils, believing in their ability to learn new skills and make the most of the opportunities offered. We cannot always guarantee outcomes but we do give opportunities for our pupils to learn about the communication of emotions and physical feelings in an appropriate and socially acceptable manner and to learn about problem solving skills and processes.

The programme still runs, and continues to change with the needs of the pupils and the school. I believe that what is important is that we continue to develop and do not forget that it is not what we do that is of greatest importance, but *how* we do it.

## References

Jordan, R.R. & Powell, S.D. (1995) *Understanding and Teaching Children with Autism.* Chichester: Wiley.

Powell, S.D. & Jordan, R.R. (1992) 'Remediating the thinking of pupils with autism:

principles into practice'. *Journal of Autism and Developmental Disorders,* **22,** 413–418.

Powell, S.D. & Jordan, R.R. (1993) 'Being subjective about autistic thinking and learning to learn'. *Educational Psychology,* **13,** 359–370.

Sinclair, J. (1992) 'A personal perspective', in E. Schopler & G.B. Mesibov (eds) *High Functioning Individuals with Autism.* New York: Plenum Press.

# COMMENTARY

## Analysing Activities

In answering his own question about why one should engage in outdoor pursuits with children with autism, Evans makes the point, which may also apply in other areas of the curriculum: that individuals with autism may be generally better at some activities than their non-autistic peers. In one sense, of course, this is not surprising. But what is interesting to consider is what there is about certain tasks that makes them amenable to the autistic way of thinking and behaving. Evans' analysis of the way in which activities such as rock climbing require little use of language, a clear and tangible route through to a goal, are logically sequenced and give individuals space and a sense of freedom, highlights how activities can be chosen which inherently meet some of the special needs mentioned earlier in this book. Such an analysis may cause a re-think of one's initial view of what is appropriate for certain individuals and what is not. It is not simply a matter of generally adopting high expectations as a matter of faith but rather as a result of a careful task (activity) analysis.

## Learning about Emotions

We argue in the opening chapters of this book that it may be necessary in autism to look carefully at the salience of learning situations for individuals and that contexts which are highly emotionally salient might well be productive situations in which to teach about emotions as well as to teach other things. Evans points to the way in which this may work in practice when he describes pupils learning to 'identify emotions, label them appropriately and then go on to learn to manage them'. Rock climbing in his conception becomes more than learning about particular physical skills; it becomes a context in which pupils can experience in an acute sense and learn to reflect on that experience. What is being described here is part therapy and part teaching and this may be indicative of a synthesis between these modes of operation which is perhaps a necessary part of education in autism (see Powell and Jordan, in press, for a fuller discussion).

## Achieving a Balance

It is a truism that the art of successful teaching is in large part a matter of providing problem solving at a level where solutions are attainable by the student but only with an amount of intellectual or physical effort (and judging the amount for each individual in each task is perhaps a significant skill in teaching). This truism becomes even more relevant in autism where individuals may have little recourse to strategies within themselves to resolve apparently insurmountable difficulties; their response to apparent failure, or an obstacle, may then be catastrophic. Evans points to the importance of balance between challenge and the already established, known ability. In autism the shifting of the balance towards tackling the unknown may need to be in smaller steps than is the case with non-autistic children but it is vitally important that the overall aim of teaching should always be to provide some challenge, even if the objective in the short term is consolidation.

The other point to consider here is that when tasks are made harder what counts as an element of increased difficulty is likely to be distinctive in autism . For example, 'help' from an adult may confound a difficulty rather than alleviate it, unless that help is focused and structured. It is here, that Evans careful teaching of the pupils to perform their own task analysis, is so important. If pupils are ever to achieve confidence in their own abilities to problem solve, they must have well-developed strategies for analysing situations, so as not to be overwhelmed by so much to be processed all at once. The teacher models the questions the pupils will eventually be taught to ask themselves so that the pupil is not just learning passive responses but active questioning techniques. This applies in classroom based as well as outdoor activities.

## Having Fun Together

Here we would like to pick up what has, somewhat unexpectedly, become something of a theme through this book; learning in pupils with autism can be greatly enhanced if the tasks chosen are highly motivating for both staff and pupils and can be enjoyed together. This seems to be the real therapeutic context in which the pupil can experience that sharing of emotion that has not occurred naturally and spontaneously in the course of early development. Of course, not all staff will be able to share the exhilaration and joy of outdoor pursuits, any more than others will share a common delight in working with a computer, as Murray describes in her chapter. It is not the outdoor activities themselves that are important (although, Evans' account demonstrates his own enthusiasm and suggests that they may be a particularly good context for the furtherance of many aspects of development), as Evans explains, but the principles and the aims that underlie them. There will be little to be gained if the unwilling teacher frog-marches his or her pupils up and down hills on the assumption that somehow this will 'do them good'. Nor is it sufficient (whatever the vagaries of our climate) to 'down tools' at the first sign of sunshine in favour of a walk in the countryside. As Evans shows so well, maximum benefit will only come when activities are carefully planned, designed to meet individual needs, and enjoyed by all the participants – pupils and staff.

## References

Powell, S.D. & Jordan, R.R. (in press) 'Education and therapy: a new synthesis in autism', in P. Shattock & G. Lindfoot (eds) *Proceeding of Autism Research Conference: Therapeutic Interventions Durham.* Sunderland: University of Sunderland/NAS.

# INDEX